THE PAGAN GOD

The Pagan God

Popular Religion in the Greco-Roman Near East

By Javier Teixidor

Princeton University Press
Princeton, New Jersey

Copyright © 1977 by Princeton University Press

Published by Princeton University Press, Princeton, New Jersey
In the United Kingdom: Princeton University Press,
Guildford, Surrey

Library of Congress Cataloging in Publication Data will
be found on the last printed page of this book

Published with the aid of The Paul Mellon Fund at
Princeton University Press

This book has been composed in Linotype Baskerville

Printed in the United States of America
by Princeton University Press, Princeton, New Jersey

To Hind Shuman

CONTENTS

CONTENTS

ILLUSTRATIONS

The Plan of Palmyra, drawn by James M. Heyle, is based on the plans of the archaeological remains published by J. Starcky in *Palmyre* (Paris: A. Maisonneuve, 1952), pp. 23–24, and by M. Gawlikowski in *Le temple palmyrénien*, Palmyre, VI (Warsaw: Université de Varsovie, Centre d'archéologie méditerranéenne, 1973), pp. 11 and 13. For some contour lines and areas 10 and 11 the writer's own photographs and drawings were used. The outline of area 4 is based on P. Collart and J. Vicari, *Le sanctuaire de Baalshamin à Palmyre*, Vol. II: *Topographie et architecture: Illustrations*, Bibliotheca helvetica romana, X (Neuchâtel: P. Attinger, 1969).

PREFACE

This book is an essay on religion in antiquity. It represents an attempt to study the religious elements which late northwestern Semitic inscriptions had in common. This epigraphical material of the second half of the first millennium B.C. *and of the first centuries* A.D., *which was recovered in the Near East during the past hundred years, is for the most part complex and at times hermetic; therefore, looking for unifying religious topics among thousands of texts may appear pointless. But a frequent perusal of Phoenician and Aramaic texts has made me discover in them a coherent body of data which is likely to be overlooked in only occasional contacts with them. The inscriptions speak for themselves, even though their message frequently comes out incomplete; I have preferred to present them as they are, without taking the shortcut of using literary texts to fill in empty spaces or to remedy deficiencies.*

The essay was planned and partly drafted while I was teaching Hellenistic religions at Columbia University. To have dealt with such a topic without making continuous references to biblical books, Gnostic movements, or the omnipresent cult of Mithra may be judged unorthodox. Pertinent information about these subjects was duly given in the classroom but was deliberately omitted from the present book because I wanted to emphasize the inscriptions themselves. Thus, the book focuses attention on firsthand data which are usually left out of manuals on the history of the religion of the Greco-Roman Near East.

I was able to discover, edit, or restudy in the museums some of the inscriptions analyzed here with the help of two institutions to which I extend my gratitude: the American Philosophical Society (during the summers of 1969 and 1970) and the American Council of Learned Societies (summer of 1972). But if the archaeological research and the work in the field were indispensable for the elaboration of my ideas, no less helpful was the discussion of the texts with the students. I hope they will benefit from the book as much as I benefited from their remarks.

In preparing my manuscript I received the skillful assistance of Miss Agnes D. Peters, to whom I want to express my gratitude.

THE PAGAN GOD

ONE

POPULAR RELIGION IN THE GRECO-ROMAN NEAR EAST

To say that history interprets the past means that the scientific methods used by the historian—and not only the conclusions he has reached in his research—will be revised periodically because each era has its own way of writing history. The historian, while writing, changes emphases because fashions of thinking also change. This is particularly true in the study of ancient civilizations, for ancient texts and monuments—or relics of them—can portray only a small portion of the civilization in which those texts and monuments were produced, and this partial knowledge of the historical truth can be suddenly challenged by new archaeological findings. To be sure, there should be no conflict between a critically examined text and a well-established archaeological fact. Therefore, occasional attempts by historians to minimize the importance of one or the other, or to produce an artificial harmony between texts and archaeological remains, should be disregarded as deceptive.[1]

Historians of Near Eastern religions during the Greco-Roman period have too often disregarded the religious inscriptions made by devotees of various Semitic extractions. Instead, they have directed their attention exclusively to the archaeological relics of those areas where the inscriptions

Note: Certain abbreviations, *ANET*, *CISem.*, *KAI*, BES, *BASOR*, *Suppl. DB*, *Dédicaces*, introduce entries in the Archaeological and Literary Sources and are also fully identified when they first occur in the footnotes; thereafter they are used throughout the notes, without subsequent identification, in the contracted forms thus established.

[1] See the important article of R. de Vaux, "On Right and Wrong Uses of Archaeology," in *Near Eastern Archaeology in the Twentieth Century*, ed. J. A. Sanders (New York: Doubleday, 1970), pp. 64–78.

were found. Furthermore, it has been customary among them to stress the value of the archaeological discoveries by quoting literary sources to such an extent that classical writers have become the sole guides in matters of religion. The result is that modern historians always point out that there was a widespread demand for new forms of religion during the post-Alexandrine centuries. The demand was indeed felt throughout the Levant and found expression especially in the tendency to turn to mystery cults. Here, the studies of A. D. Nock[2] and F. Cumont[3] may be of great help in the consideration of this particularly complex chapter of the history of religion. It is not enough, however, to describe the emergence of initiatory procedures, the popularity of the Orphic or Dionysiac rites, the prominence of the cult of Isis, or even the impact of Mithraism in the Levant, for these religious phenomena tell us little about the feelings of the broad masses. It is in the copious inscriptions produced by the Semites in their own homeland or abroad that paramount interest lies.

The inscriptions rarely convey the impression that the popular piety was undermined by Hellenistic culture. Unfortunately, this evidence has been neglected by modern scholars. Nock openly admitted that he was not interested in the life of the undeveloped countryside.[4] As a result of this attitude a fictitious image of the contemporary Near Eastern pieties emerges. To discuss the immortality of the soul or how to acquire the true gnosis were not popular

[2] See Nock's books *Conversion* (Fair Lawn, N.J.: Oxford University Press, 1961) and *Early Gentile Christianity and Its Hellenistic Background* (New York: Harper and Row, Harper Torchbooks, 1964). Under the latter title are collected essays published in 1928 and 1952.

[3] F. Cumont, *Les religions orientales dans le paganisme romain*, 4th ed. (Paris: Paul Geuthner, 1929). It is unfortunate that the English translation, *Oriental Religions in Roman Paganism* (reprint ed., New York: Dover Publications, 1956), has been made from the edition of 1911.

[4] Nock, *Early Gentile Christianity*, p. 3.

concerns. It is certain that the safety of the soul in the afterlife was studied by Greek and Latin writers all the way from the fifth century B.C. to the fourth century A.D. Socrates, at one end of the span, declares that the immortality of the soul is a doctrine "true" and "fine";[5] at the other end, the Emperor Julian, in his *Letter to a Priest*, professes the same conviction.[6] The common man, however, never rose above his daily prayers, and we may wonder with Harnack whether the mystery religions were ever the actual creed of the unenlightened faithful. On the contrary, Harnack claims that the mysteries may in fact have confused the masses "by casting obstacles in the way of their access to a rational religion."[7] The conclusion that major changes had taken place in the Near East during the centuries preceding Christianity was drawn from Classical writers in order to present Christianity as the legitimate answer to man's anguish. Most of the books dealing with the subject are in fact apologetics, but apologetics is not the best of the gifts which were handed down to European civilization by early Christian writers.

Near Eastern religions maintained their traditional character during the last centuries of the first millennium B.C., as is conclusively attested by innumerable inscriptions. Religion in the Near East was not subjected to the challenge of speculative and critical thought which influenced the daily life of Greece during the third century B.C. In general,

[5] A number of Platonic dialogues deal with immortality and reincarnation, but Plato's statements on these subjects are not altogether clear. However difficult a formulation of his doctrine of immortality might be, it is certain that according to Socrates the philosopher's task consisted in knowing the Truth, thus allowing his soul to free itself from the body and participate in immortality.

[6] Julian *Epistulae* 298D–299A; trans. W. C. Wright, Loeb Classical Library (Cambridge, Mass., 1969), II, pp. 320–322.

[7] A. Harnack, *The Mission and Expansion of Christianity in the First Three Centuries*, trans. and ed. J. Moffatt (New York: Harper and Row, Harper Torchbooks, 1962), p. 237.

the temper of Near Eastern religions is more satisfactorily felt by reading the religious inscriptions than by, say, the literary sarcasms of Lucian of Samosata.

Popular religion must have remained practically unchanged in Greco-Roman times, for the inscriptions do not reflect the impact of new fashions. The cult of the Lord of Heaven and the epithets applied to him, the reverence for holy places or baetyls, the various types of sacrifices, the widespread use of altars, the religious "associations" or "brotherhoods" that existed everywhere,[8] all this was preserved through generations from the time of the Persian empire down to the first Christian centuries. By definition this form of religiosity is traditional or unhistoric, and no theological creed, such as appears in Judaism or Christianity, can ever be found here.[9] The faithful were intuitive and simple; occasionally their practices reflect a bourgeois contentment, for instance, in the hundreds of texts that end by saying that the offering was made "because the god has listened to the prayer." This idea in particular is worth developing.

---

[8] The terms to indicate these religious or professional associations are *mrzḥ* and *ḥbr*; the first was very much in use among the Nabataeans and at Palmyra, where the president of the *thiasus* is called *rb mrzḥ'*. For the term *ḥbr* at Hatra, see J. Teixidor, *Sumer* 20 (1964), 77. J. T. Milik has studied in detail these religious associations in *Dédicaces faites par des dieux* (hereafter *Dédicaces*), chs. iv and v, and pp. 392–393, a work published as volume i of *Recherches d'épigraphie proche-orientale*, Bibliothèque archéologique et historique, xcii (Paris: Paul Geuthner, 1972). The presence of the term *mrzḥ* in Amos 6:7 and Jeremiah 16:5 prompted the studies of O. Eissfeldt in *Syria* 43 (1966), 39–47, and *Oriens antiquus* 5 (1966), 165–176 (republished in his *Kleine Schriften*, iv [Tübingen: Mohr, 1968], pp. 264–270 and 285–296). I have reviewed these articles in "Bulletin d'épigraphie sémitique" (hereafter BES; in *Syria* from 1967 on) 1971, no. 24.

[9] In Judaism one may recall the summaries of sacred history recorded in Deuteronomy 6:20–24 and 26:5–9. For creedal elements in the Early Church, see J.N.D. Kelly, *Early Christian Creeds*, 3rd ed. (New York: David McKay, 1972), chs. 1 and 2.

Friendly Gods and Contented Believers

In Apuleius's novel *The Golden Ass* Lucius, weary of the life of an ass, called upon Isis, and the goddess went to his aid. The divine response to human prayers was a fact acknowledged by the worshipers of the Oriental gods, whom they often styled in Greek as *epekooi*, i.e., the ones who listen to prayers. Thus, the story of a goddess granting her favor to a believer must have been not only enjoyed but believed by many readers all over the Greco-Roman Near East and Punic North Africa. Apuleius was certainly a man with a definite taste for religious feeling and knew what religious faith was, even though the Emperor Septimius Severus may have thought that his book was "a Punic Milesian phantasy."[10] In his novel *Icaromenippus* Lucian of Samosata, a contemporary of Apuleius, mocked the belief that the gods listen to human prayers. His sarcasm, however, confirms how widespread the belief in the *theoi epekooi* was. In the novel Menippus is described as going with Zeus "to the place where Zeus had to sit and hear the prayers. There was a row of openings like mouths of wells, with covers on them, and beside each stood a golden throne. Sitting down by the first one, Zeus took off the cover and gave his attention to the people who were praying. The prayers came from all parts of the world and were of all sorts and kinds, for I myself [i.e., Menippus] bent over the orifice and listened to them along with him. They went like this: 'O Zeus, may I succeed in becoming king!' 'O Zeus, make my onions and my garlic grow!' 'O ye gods, let my father die quickly!'; and now and then one or another would say: 'O that I may inherit my wife's property!' 'O that I may be undetected in my plot against my brother!' 'May I succeed in winning my suit!' 'Let me win the wreath at the Olympic games!' Among seafaring men, one was praying for the north wind to blow, another for the south

---

[10] *Scriptores historiae augustae*: Capitolinus *Clodius Albinus* 12: 12.

7

wind; and the farmers were praying for rain while the washermen were praying for sunshine."[11]

Late Phoenician and Aramaic inscriptions do not specify the various needs of believers as Lucian does, of course, but in some instances the inscriptions record that offerings were made because the god had heard the voices of the believers. This practice is attested as early as the ninth century B.C. in the Aramaic inscription of Bar-Hadad, who set up a stele in honor of Melqart.[12] In a Phoenician inscription of the fifth century B.C. Yeḥawmilk, king of Byblos, says explicitly that he invoked the Lady of Byblos and she heard him.[13] Phoenician inscriptions found at Kition, on Cyprus, style Astarte as the goddess who listens to prayers, and a few inscriptions from Idalion, to be dated to the fourth century B.C., honor Reshef for the same reason.[14] In a text of the second century B.C. from Malta two brothers, probably natives of Tyre, made vows to Melqart because he had heard their prayers.[15] Pious Semites living in Delos give

[11] Lucian of Samosata *Icaromenippus* ch. 25; trans. A. M. Harmon, Loeb Classical Library (Cambridge, Mass., 1961), II, p. 311.

[12] *Ancient Near Eastern Texts Relating to the Old Testament* (hereafter *ANET*), ed. James B. Pritchard, 2nd ed. (Princeton: Princeton University Press, 1955), p. 501. Text and German translation in H. Donner and W. Röllig, *Kanaanäische und aramäische Inschriften* (hereafter *KAI*), 3 vols. (I, 2nd ed., Wiesbaden: Otto Harrassowitz; II, 2nd ed., ibid., 1968; III, 1964), no. 201 and II, pp. 203–204. F. M. Cross has published a new reading of the text in the *Bulletin of the American Schools of Oriental Research* (hereafter *BASOR*), no. 205 (Feb. 1972), 36–42, but his interpretation of the second line remains very hypothetical.

[13] *ANET*, p. 502; *KAI* 10.

[14] Kition: *KAI* 32. Idalion: *KAI* 38, 39; cf. 41. For the cult of Reshef on Cyprus, see Teixidor, BES 1969, nos. 85–86; BES 1970, no. 69. D. Conrad has published an exhaustive study of the god in the ancient Near East in *Zeitschrift für die Alttestamentliche Wissenschaft* 83 (1971), 157–183.

[15] *KAI* 47. M. G. Guzzo Amadasi (*Le iscrizioni fenicie e puniche delle colonie in occidente*, Studi semitici, 28 [Rome: Istituto di studi del Vicino Oriente, 1967]) wrongly states that the epithet of Melqart, *b'l ṣr*,

the epithet *epekooi* to the gods of Ascalon and the Egyptian gods, and also to Apollo.[16] Similar expressions of gratitude are found in the Hauran inscriptions where *epekoos* was an epithet of Baal Shamin exclusively.[17] In Hellenistic Ptolemaïs, in Palestine, Hadad and Atargatis are invoked as *theoi epekooi*.[18] This is also the epithet of the so-called "anonymous" god of Palmyra, who in Palmyrene inscriptions is styled *raḥmana wetayara*, i.e., the compassionate and merciful one, and in Greek inscriptions is given the epithet *epekoos*.[19] A Palmyrene of the third century of our era invoked the "anonymous" god everywhere, and apparently, from what he says on a votive altar, the god always heard the prayers of this fortunate man.[20] Another Palmyrene discloses that, in distress, he called on the "anonymous" god and the god set him free, a phrase that clearly matches the feelings of the author of Psalm 118:5.[21] This Semitic piety is well illustrated in the book of Jonah. According to the author of the book, the king of Nineveh proclaimed a general fast in his city, hoping that God would repent and turn away from his fierce anger against the Ninevites. Jonah

---

was used to form theophoric names in North Africa (her p. 16); see Teixidor, BES 1971, no. 40.

[16] P. Bruneau, *Recherches sur les cultes de Délos à l'époque hellénistique et à l'époque impériale*, Bibliothèque des écoles françaises d'Athènes et de Rome, fasc. 217 (Paris: E. de Boccard, 1970), p. 167.

[17] D. Sourdel, *Les cultes du Hauran à l'époque romaine* (Paris: Paul Geuthner, 1952), pp. 26 and 98.

[18] M. Avi-Yonah, "Syrian Gods at Ptolemais-Accho," *Israel Exploration Journal* 9 (1959), 1–12. For the cults of the city, see Chapter Two below.

[19] See Chapter Four.

[20] The text says that he invoked the god *by sea and by land*; see *Corpus inscriptionum semiticarum* (hereafter *CISem.*), II, 4047. The expression "to invoke him everywhere" is also attested; see *CISem.*, II, 4011.

[21] Dj. al-Hassani and J. Starcky, "Autels palmyréniens découverts près de la source Efca," *Annales archéologiques de Syrie* 3 (1953), 160–163.

himself plainly acknowledges his reason for running away to Tarshish was that, knowing that God is merciful and gracious, he did not want to see his prophecies of doom fail to be fulfilled.[22]

In these Semitic societies the gods were supposed to look after their worshipers, and as a result the believers themselves felt a rather unusual degree of solidarity with their gods. Inscriptions from Palmyra, Hatra, and Tyre, dating from the beginning of our era, commemorate occasional honors granted by the gods to their devotees. At times, as in Palmyra, the gods together with the representatives of the important tribes even erected statues to prominent citizens. In Hatra, gods alone honored believers with statues.[23] An inscription from Hatra and another from Umm el-'Ammed, near Tyre, indicate that the gods shared with mortals the responsibility for building a temple to a major divinity.[24]

This relationship seems to mirror a society of well-to-do citizens at peace with their gods. The material prosperity of Palmyra was particularly conspicuous during the second century of our era, and the city reached the peak of her glory when Hadrian visited her in 131. An inscription from these golden days commemorates an offering made to the "anonymous" god and to 'iddana ṭaba, i.e., "the good, or happy, age." With this phrase the Palmyrenes meant to personify the golden age as a goddess, a type of cult that seems close to that of the Roman *Felicitas saeculi* which appeared on the coins of Marcus Aurelius and Lucius Verus from 161 onward.[25]

---

[22] See E. Bickerman, *Four Strange Books of the Bible* (New York: Schocken Books, 1967), pp. 3–49. The author gives the title "Jonah or the Unfulfilled Prophecy" to his essay on the book of Jonah. G. Steiner (*After Babel: Aspects of Language and Translation* [New York: Oxford University Press paperback, 1976], p. 147) rightly describes the tale of Jonah as an "intellectual comedy."

[23] Milik, *Dédicaces*, pp. 324–353.   [24] Ibid., ch. VIII.

[25] J. Cantineau, "Tadmorea 13: la bonne époque," *Syria* 14 (1933), 192–193.

The inscriptions are far from reflecting any feeling of insecurity or a peremptory need of salvation. The faithful simply expected the gods to listen to their prayers. It was this traditional confidence that made pagan religion so popular.

TRADITIONAL RELIGION

One of the main issues in the polemic between Celsus and Origen[26] is precisely that Christianity is not traditional, that is to say, that Christianity appeared with Jesus. Celsus defended tradition, believing that "it is impious to abandon the customs which have existed in each locality from the beginning" (5. 25). Of course, from his viewpoint to accept Jesus as a redeemer sent by God could not but raise serious doubts about the legitimacy of the Christian faith. To a religious pagan the whole concept of a new religion was absurd. A poignant question raised by Celsus against his adversary was: "Is it only now after such a long age that God has remembered to judge the human race? Did He not care before?" (4. 8). Origen naturally left the question unanswered. To obviate this kind of objection from the philosophers, Justin, a few decades before Origen was born, had presented Jesus as "the teacher" (1 *Apology* 4). He drew a parallel between Jesus' doctrine and that of Socrates, who had also tried to enlighten men by true reasoning (1 *Apology* 5). To Justin, however, Jesus was the incarnate Reason of God and consequently his preaching was the true philosophy that deals with perennial truths. Expanding the same idea, Tertullian claimed in *De anima* 2. 4 that Christianity had enhanced human capabilities. In general, the apologists postulated that the Greek philosophers owed whatever truth they discovered to the biblical prophets from whom they had derived it. In this sense Christianity

[26] I have followed the translation of H. Chadwick, *Origen: Contra Celsum* (Cambridge: At the University Press, 1965). The work is to be dated to A.D. 248; see Chadwick's remarks in pp. xiv–xv.

11

for the apologists ought to be considered not an innovative doctrine but the fulfillment of what some philosophers had already initiated.

The religion to which Celsus refers had a long tradition, and the political unity of the Near East helped to preserve it. This religious and political unity is wrongly believed to have started with Alexander's conquest of the Near East. In fact, well before the Greeks, the Persians had formed an empire which extended from the Indus to Ethiopia. The political unity of the Achaemenid empire was stable and the immense territory remained uniformly inspected by officers who called themselves "the eye of the king."[27] After the Persians, Alexander governed his empire in accordance with Persian traditions, thus bridging the differences between himself as a Macedonian and the previous Asiatic monarchs. With the Greeks the unity seems to have been reinforced rather than initiated. Alexander's aim at a universal monarchy was supported by the fact that the conception of divinity had become more spiritualized and many local cults lost their exclusiveness and welcomed foreigners.[28] But this spiritual unification had already started with

[27] R. N. Frye, *The Heritage of Persia* (London: Weidenfeld and Nicolson, 1965), p. 102. A. L. Oppenheim has made important remarks about this institution in the Persian empire in his article "The Eyes of the Lord," *Journal of the American Oriental Society* 88 (1968), 173–180; see especially pp. 173 and 178.

[28] This becomes obvious through the widespread use of the term *ger* in theophoric names. The original meaning of the term in Hebrew was "resident alien," and after Nehemiah's time it came to mean "proselyte"; see M. Smith, *Palestinian Parties and Politics That Shaped the Old Testament* (New York: Columbia University Press, 1971), pp. 178–182. Phoenician personal names of the type *Gereshmun*, "proselyte of Eshmun," *Gerastarte*, "proselyte of Astarte," etc., are well attested in the inscriptions; see Teixidor, BES 1968, no. 73; BES 1970, no. 20, and BES 1972, no. 109. Also F. L. Benz, *Personal Names in the Phoenician and Punic Inscriptions* (Rome: Biblical Institute Press, 1972), p. 298. At Madāin Ṣāliḥ, in Nabataean territory, *gr* is used to indicate the female dependents ("clients" or "protégées") of Wushoh's family; see *CISem.*, II, 205; A. J. Jaussen and R. Savignac, *Mission archéologique en*

the Persians. It is reported that in his first regnal year Cyrus allowed the Jews to build their temple at Jerusalem and practice their faith. He showed great benevolence to all foreign gods. In 539 B.C., when he entered Babylonia, he reestablished in their temples the gods displaced by Nabonidus. In the Babylonian documents, which record the sojourn of Cyrus at Babylon, modern readers can discover a well-planned propaganda intended to flatter his new subjects.[29] Primarily, this propaganda was to ease the recognition of all the local cults; fortuitously, it promoted an atmosphere in which monotheism could flourish.

PAGAN MONOTHEISM

Monotheism had always been latent among the Semites. Though much has been written on the subject, for the purpose of this study it is adequate to say that in the second half of the first millennium B.C. a certain monotheistic spirit permeated Near Eastern inscriptions. This, to a great extent, is the conclusion to be drawn from the fact that the "assemblies of gods" vanish in the epigraphical material. The preeminence of the supreme god in the ancient pantheons of Mesopotamia or Ugarit was often overshadowed

---

Arabie, I (Paris: E. Leroux, 1909), pp. 162–165, no. 12. At Palmyra the meaning of *gr* is either that of "guest" (for instance, *CISem.*, II, 3972: Atenatan offered a stele to the god Šadrafa "in order to become a votary in his temple") or that of "host," i.e., not the receiver but the giver of the hospitality (see the inscription of a Nabataean horseman at Palmyra in G. A. Cooke, *A Text-Book of North-Semitic Inscriptions* [Oxford: Clarendon Press, 1903], pp. 303–305, no. 140B). This latter use of the term is fully confirmed by a personal name such as *Kosgeros*, "[the god] Kos is host," found at Memphis; see M. Lidzbarski, *Ephemeris für semitische Epigraphik*, II (Giessen: A. Töpelmann, 1908), pp. 340–341, and J. G. Milne, *Greek Inscriptions*, Service des antiquités de l'Égypte, Catalogue général des antiquités égyptiennes du Musée du Caire (Oxford: Oxford University Press, 1905), pp. 35–37, no. 9283.

[29] A. T. Olmstead, *History of the Persian Empire* (Chicago: University of Chicago Press, 1948), pp. 51–56.

by the presence of divine assemblies wherein minor gods, by their maneuverings, could occasionally hinder the decision of the chief god of the pantheon. Divine assemblies survived in the pantheons of Karatepe or Byblos until Persian times, according to the Phoenician inscriptions found there.[30] However, from the fourth century B.C onward the inscriptions no longer acknowledged the existence of these divine assemblies. Instead, devotion to angels, or overseers, or messengers of the god (usually a supreme one) gained ground in pagan circles. It is interesting to find that the *Book of Enoch*[31] called the angels "the holy sons of God" in much the same way that the Karatepe inscription invoked "the whole family of the children of the gods."

The cult of the angels sets up a new trend in ancient Near Eastern religiosity. At Palmyra Semitic inscriptions mention the "Angel of Bel" (Malakbel) and the "Holy Brothers" or "Holy Angels" of Baal Shamin. The "Angels

[30] The inscription of Karatepe (which I date to the ninth century B.C.; see BES 1971, no. 98) refers to "the whole family (*kl dr*) of the children of the gods" (see *KAI* 26); an inscription from Byblos of the ninth century B.C. mentions "the assembly (*mphrt*) of the holy gods of Byblos" (see *KAI* 4). The Phoenician amulet of Arslan Tash (seventh century B.C.) follows the Karatepe text in invoking "the great (ones) of the council (*dr*) of all the holy ones"; see F. M. Cross and R. J. Saley, *BASOR*, no. 197 (Feb. 1970), 45. In Hellenistic times, the concept of the divine assemblies seems to fade away, while that of the *family of the gods* is being nurtured by the faithful. Simultaneously the Oriental gods become the *holy ones* (the Greek *agios* must have rendered the Semitic *qodesh*); see Cumont, *Religions orientales*, p. 260, note 65. It is interesting to note that a stele of Astarte found in the region of Tyre bears an inscription invoking the goddess as the one "who [dwells] amidst the community of the saints (*bgw hqdš*)"; see J. T. Milik, *Biblica* 48 (1967), 572–573.

[31] The book was probably composed during the second century and the first third of the first century B.C.; see R. H. Charles, *The Apocrypha and Pseudepigrapha of the Old Testament*, II (Oxford Clarendon Press, 1966), pp. 170–171. See new remarks about the date of composition in O. Eissfeldt, *The Old Testament: An Introduction*, English trans. P. R. Ackroyd from the 3rd German ed. (New York: Harper and Row, 1965), pp. 617–622.

of Holiness" of Emesa were venerated at Coptos. The people of Umm el-'Ammed, near Tyre, revered the "Angel" of Milk-astart. J. T. Milik, who has studied this epigraphical material extensively,[32] has read the name *Idaruma*, the angel of the Nabataean god Dushara, in a Greek inscription from the Hauran.[33] The same writer interprets the Greek *mal-ache(l)aleian* of a Ma'lula inscription of A.D. 107 as meaning *mal'ak 'el-'aliyan*, i.e., the "Angel of god the Most High."[34]

This cult, however, did not stand in the way of monotheism. Nor, for that matter, did the cult of many gods prevent belief in a supreme divine being. Monotheism did not, of course, originate in a profound religious experience but in theological thought to which the political unity of the Near East under Persians and Greeks gave an adequate frame. Whether the term "god" was used for one or for many holy beings is irrelevant; what matters is that the power of one being was believed to prevail over the others' power. Belief in a supreme god is acknowledged in the inscriptions, as will be seen in the following chapters. Together with the acceptance of a god of the Zeus type, the faithful revered other gods who were their sponsors in some of their concrete enterprises or needs. This simultaneous fidelity to both a supreme god and other "specialized" gods in charge of specific functions in the world stresses the religious unity of the Near East rather than dissolves it. Plutarch, born in A.D. 46, accused the Stoics of having changed these "deputy" gods into natural forces. He clearly states the reality of their personalities: "We must not make them unable to go out, like the queens in a hive of bees, nor keep them imprisoned by enclosing them with matter, or rather fencing them about with it, as those do who make the gods to be atmospheric conditions, or regard them as powers of waters or of fire blended therewith, and bring them into being at the same time with the world, and burn them up with it, since they are not unconfined and free

[32] Milik, *Dédicaces*, pp. 423–427.   [33] Ibid., p. 428.
[34] Ibid., p. 433.

like drivers of horses or pilots of ships, but, just as statues are riveted and welded to their bases, so they are enclosed and fastened to the corporeal. . . . That other concept is, I think, more dignified and sublime, that the gods are not subject to outside control, but are their own masters, even as the twin sons of Tyndareus come to the aid of men who are labouring in the storm . . . not, however, sailing on the ships and sharing in the danger, but appearing above and rescuing; so, in the same way, one or another of the gods visits now this world and now that, led thither by pleasure in the sight, and co-operates with Nature in the direction of each."[35]

This remarkable text is, of course, to be understood within Plutarch's philosophy, and it should not be considered a testimony in favor of popular beliefs. The text, however, helps the modern man understand the belief in the presence of these "deputy" gods to whom offerings were made. Celsus also maintained the duty of living by ancestral usages and saw in the doctrine affirming that "only one being has been called Lord" an impious way of dividing the kingdom of God. There are no factions: there is a world in which "anyone," he says, "who honours and worships all those who belong to him does not hurt God at all, since they are all his" (8. 10-11).[36] A plurality of cults did not corrode the feeling of unity which had developed under the unifying political power of Persians and Greeks. Celsus openly admitted that "each nation follows its traditional customs, whatever kind may happen to be established. This situation seems to have come to pass not only because it came into the head of different people to think differently . . . but also because it is probable that from the beginning the different parts of the earth were allotted to different overseers, and are governed in this way by having been divided between certain authorities" (5. 25).[37]

[35] Plutarch *De defectu oraculorum* 426BC; trans. F. C. Babbitt, Loeb Classical Library (Cambridge, Mass., 1962). v, p. 437.
[36] Origen *Contra Celsum*; trans. Chadwick, pp. 459–460.
[37] Ibid., p. 283.

Inscriptions and coins mention the names, and portray the images, of the gods whose cults were relevant to the populace of the Greco-Roman Near East. The epigraphical material reveals that the worship of a supreme god co-existed with that of other minor gods. The belief that one god is able to control all the other gods, or is supreme in that he has created and looks after the world does not constitute monotheism. But the increasing emphasis on such beliefs is evidence of a trend toward monotheism, namely toward the exclusion of other gods' existence. In the Near East of Greco-Roman times this trend facilitated the spread of Judaism, Christianity, and Islam. Conversely, monotheism could take a form very close to belief in a supreme deity. In his *Sociology of Religion* Max Weber concludes that only Judaism and Islam are strictly monotheistic in principle because the Christian trinitarianism as well as the Catholic cult of the saints make Christianity come fairly close to polytheism, at least close to the Greco-Roman practices of the Near East when the devotion to youthful gods, or to divine messengers, fulfilled the imagination and the feelings of the masses.

MAP I

Syro-Phoenicia and Palestine

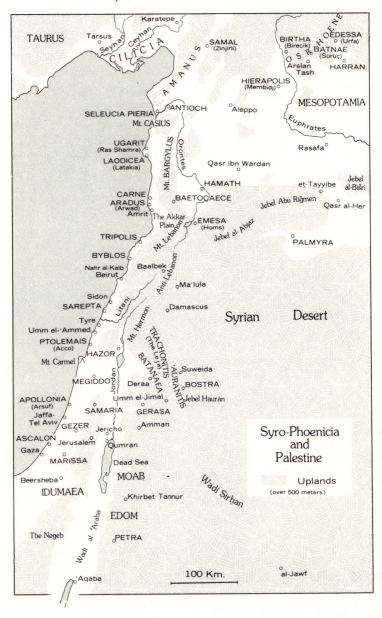

TAURUS

Karatepe

Tarsus

Seyhan

Ceyhan

C I L I C I A

A M A N U S

SAMAL
(Zinjirli)

OSRHOENE

BIRTHA
(Birecik)

EDESSA
(Urfa)

BATNAE
(Sürüç)

Arslan
Tash

HARRAN

HIERAPOLIS
(Membidj)

MESOPOTAMIA

SELEUCIA PIERIA

ANTIOCH

Aleppo

Mt. CASIUS

Euphrates

Orontes

Mt. BARGYLUS

UGARIT
(Ras Shamra)

Qasr ibn Wardan

Rasafa

LAODICEA
(Latakia)

HAMATH

et-Tayyibe

Jebel
al-Bišri

CARNE
ARADUS
(Arwad)

BAETOCAECE

Jebel Abu Riğmen

Qasr al-Her

Amrit

The Akkar
Plain

EMESA
(Homs)

Jebel al-Abjaz

TRIPOLIS

Mt. Lebanon

PALMYRA

BYBLOS

Baalbek

Nahr al-Kalb

Beirut

Anti-Lebanon

Ma'lula

Sidon

SAREPTA

Litani

Mt. Hermon

Damascus

Syrian

Desert

Tyre

Umm el-'Ammed

PTOLEMAIS
(Acco)

HAZOR

TRACHONITIS
(The Leja)

BATANAEA

AURANITIS

Mt. Carmel

Suweida

MEGIDDO

Jordan

Deraa

BOSTRA

Jebel Hauran

APOLLONIA
(Arsuf)

Umm el-Jimal

Jaffa-
Tel Aviv

SAMARIA

GERASA

GEZER

Jericho

Amman

ASCALON

Jerusalem

Qumran

Gaza

MARISSA

Dead Sea

Syro-Phoenicia
and
Palestine

Beersheba

MOAB

Uplands
(over 500 meters)

IDUMAEA

Khirbet Tannur

Wadi Sirḥan

The Negeb

EDOM

Wadi al. 'Araba

PETRA

Aqaba

100 Km.

al-Jawf

TWO

PHOENICIAN AND SYRIAN DEITIES

HERODOTUS and Thucydides present the Phoenicians as a
well-defined ethnic group, but so does the *Iliad* a few centuries earlier. The Homeric epic identifies Phoenicians and
Sidonians and describes them as craftsmen and navigators:
"At once the son of Peleus set out prizes for the foot-race:
/ a mixing-bowl of silver, a work of art, which held only /
six measures, but for its loveliness it surpassed all others
/ on earth by far, since skilled Sidonian craftsmen had
wrought it / well, and Phoenicians carried it over the
misty face of the water / and set it in the harbour, and
gave it for a present to Thoas."[1]

The reference to Phoenician skill both in metalworking
and in sailing for the purpose of trading fits in with the
culture of the Levant in the eighth century B.C.[2] But the
Sidonians were not the only Phoenicians in the Levant. Between Mount Casius, in the north, and Mount Carmel,
in the south, the Syro-Palestinian coast was populated by
Phoenicians. We know that their most important towns
were Aradus, Byblos, Berytus, Sidon, Tyre, and Acco. Yet
it is difficult to say when Phoenician history starts. The date
can scarcely be determined by the sporadic presence of Near
Eastern artifacts in the Aegean or the western Mediterranean area, for this leaves open the question of when such
objects became distinctively "Phoenician." Nor is it of much
help to learn from late biblical texts that the Phoenician
city of Tyre became a commercial power in the tenth cen-

---

[1] *Iliad* 23. 740–745. The translation is that of R. Lattimore, *The Iliad
of Homer* (Chicago: University of Chicago Press, 1951).

[2] See the study of J. D. Muhly, "Homer and the Phoenicians," *Berytus*
19 (1970), 19–64, in particular pp. 49–52, 62–63.

tury B.C.[3] However obscure were the origins of this people, one point is clearly attested by the inscriptions they left behind: the Phoenicians spoke a language cognate to that current at Ugarit in the fourteenth and thirteenth centuries B.C. and to the common speech of the Israelites.

The evolution of Phoenician from the Canaanite language at the stage in which it appears at Ugarit must have taken place at the end of the second millennium B.C. An intermediate stage of that process of evolution is probably represented by texts inscribed on arrowheads found in southern Palestine and Lebanon; they date from the twelfth century B.C.[4] Rudimentary as they may be, these short inscriptions were already written in linear Phoenician characters; thus they belong to the period in which "the pictographic script evolved into linear."[5] To the last step of the evolution we can attribute the inscription of Ahiram of Byblos about 1000 B.C.; the Gezer inscription in Palestine, from the tenth century B.C.; the royal stele of Moab, dated from the middle of the ninth century B.C.; the inscription of Zinjirli, and maybe that of Karatepe, also from the ninth century B.C.[6] Two Phoenician inscriptions from Cyprus can be added to the group.[7]

[3] 1 Kings 9:27 presents Solomon and Hiram of Tyre as partners: "And Hiram sent with the fleet his servants, seamen who were familiar with the sea, together with the servants of Solomon." Solomon used Tyrian sailors in the same way the Old Kingdom monarchs employed the seamen of Byblos; see J. A. Montgomery, *The Books of Kings*, International Critical Commentary (Edinburgh: T. & T. Clark, 1951), p. 211.

[4] See the article of F. M. Cross, "The Origin and Early Evolution of the Alphabet," *Eretz-Israel* 8 (1967), 8*–24*, for a comprehensive presentation of the epigraphical material from Phoenicia and Palestine.

[5] Ibid., pp. 13* ff.

[6] For the inscription of Karatepe, see Teixidor, BES 1971, pp. 470–472, nos. 97–98.

[7] *KAI* 30 gives the inscription found by A. H. Honeyman in 1939. Its place of origin is unknown. The stone is badly damaged and incomplete. Seven lines remain visible, but only a few words can be satisfactorily read. These lines indicate that the inscription was funerary and that

The development of Canaanite took place under the influence of Egypt, the cultural presence of which is fully recognized by Rib-Abda, the ruler of Byblos in about 1370 B.C., who assures the Pharaoh that Byblos was as Egyptian as Memphis.[8] The same conviction is held by Zakar-Baal, the king of Byblos mentioned in the report of Wenamon. Even though this document was written at a time when Egypt was too weak to command respect in Asia, the Egyptian storyteller makes the Phoenician king admit that "when Amun founded all lands, in founding them he founded first the land of Egypt from which you come; for craftsmanship came out of it, to reach the place where I am, and learning came out of it, to reach the place where I am."[9] It is interesting to note that the table of nations of Genesis 10 gives the names of Cush, Egypt, Punt (Libya), and Canaan as those of the children of Ham. Canaan therefore appears as a young brother of Egypt. In the same vein, Sidon is considered in Genesis 10:15 the "first-born" of Canaan. Biblical tradition obviously confirms what can be gleaned from the epigraphical records.

Following the destruction of Ugarit in the thirteenth century B.C. and the sociopolitical disruptions occasioned by the invasion of the "Sea Peoples," the inhabitants of the Syro-Palestinian littoral emerged as the successors of the

---

some kind of warning was pronounced in the text against those who would attempt to destroy the tomb. The second inscription was found by V. Karageorghis at Kition in 1969. It is incised in fragments of a votive bowl. The archaeological context dates the object from the end of the ninth century B.C., a period which is in agreement with the date assigned to the inscription on paleographical grounds. The inscription was edited by A. Dupont-Sommer, *Mémoires de l'Académie des Inscriptions et Belles-Lettres* 44 (1970), but see Teixidor, BES 1972, no. 118. The text remains as yet undeciphered.

[8] See El Amarna letters nos. 84 and 139 (J. A. Knudtzon, ed., *Die El-Amarna-Tafeln*, Vorderasiatische Bibliothek, 2 [Leipzig: Hinrichs, 1915]). For the Egyptian scribes in Palestine and Phoenicia, see W. F. Albright in *ANET*, p. 484, note 2.

[9] I follow the translation published in *ANET*, pp. 25–29; see p. 27.

ancient Canaanites, and as such they were known, the name Canaanite persisting in North Africa until the days of St. Augustine.[10] To Greeks and Romans, however, the Canaanites were known as "Phoenicians." Whatever the original meaning of this term may have been,[11] it was used comprehensively to connote the non-Semitic as well as the Semitic populace of the area. Among the former were the Mycenaeans and the Philistines, peoples who blended, if only in part, with the extant Semitic communities of the coast during the last centuries of the second millennium B.C.

About 1000 B.C. the language of the inscriptions found in Syria, Palestine, and Cyprus becomes a sort of lingua franca. Linguistically, the texts of Zinjirli, Karatepe, Byblos, Gezer, or Moab were unmistakably homogeneous, although distinctive dialectal features are indeed noticeable here and there. Moreover, the style in which the events are narrated clearly manifests the tastes and manners of a common culture.

The period in question coincides with the emergence of the Aramaeans as an important factor in the politics of the Near East. A group among the West Semitic nomadic tribes, the Aramaeans were styled Akhlamu in Assyrian documents of the fourteenth century B.C.[12] In the second half of the eleventh century B.C. they gained control of large areas in the Syrian Desert and consequently of the caravan routes. Some two hundred years later, they had succeeded in forming an empire. Indirectly, this may have

[10] See Augustine *Epistulae ad Romanos inchoata expositio* 13 (Migne, *PL* xxxv, 2096). An inscription from Cirta, now Constantine, dating from the period before the Roman occupation, mentions somebody by the name of ʻAbdeshmun son of Modir, "Canaanite" (ʻš knʻn); see A. Berthier and R. Charlier, *Le sanctuaire punique d'El-Hofra à Constantine* (Paris: Arts et métiers graphiques, 1955), pp. 83–84, no. 102.

[11] Muhly, *Berytus* 19 (1970), 24 ff.

[12] B. Mazar, "The Aramaean Empire and Its Relations with Israel," in *Biblical Archaeologist*, no. xxv (Dec. 1962), 97–120.

helped the people of the coast to develop cultural features of their own as a reaction against the invading Aramaeans. For one thing, the Phoenician language held firm against the spread of Aramaic dialects from all over the Syrian interior until finally it became the language not only of the coastal cities but also of their colonies in the western Mediterranean.[13]

In the second half of the ninth century B.C., Ben-Hadad II consolidated the Aramaean kingdoms—some sixteen districts—into one state, Aram, with its capital at Damascus.[14] Meanwhile the Phoenician coastal cities maintained friendly relations with the royal houses of Israel and Judah. Architects and craftsmen of Hiram, king of Tyre, worked on the construction of the temple of Jerusalem, as is stated in 1 Kings 5. Phoenician architects also worked at Samaria, the capital of Israel founded by Omri. The buildings of the city, now ascribed to Omri's reign and to that of his successor Ahab,[15] are of a beautiful Phoenician style which can be compared with the architecture of Megiddo or Dan, at the headwaters of the Jordan,[16] and with that of Kition in

[13] Z. S. Harris, *A Grammar of the Phoenician Language* (New Haven: American Oriental Society, 1936), pp. 6–8; S. Moscati, *Problematica della civiltà fenicia*, Studi semitici, 46 (Rome: Consiglio Nazionale delle Ricerche, 1974), p. 32.

[14] Mazar as cited in note 12 above.

[15] K. Kenyon, *Archaeology in the Holy Land*, 3rd ed. (New York: Praeger, 1970), pp. 265–266, 347, and her *Royal Cities of the Old Testament* (New York: Schocken Books, 1971), pp. 76 ff.

[16] So far only preliminary reports of the excavations carried out at Dan have been published; see, for instance, *Revue biblique* 77 (1970), 383–385, and 78 (1971), 415–418. From Judges 18:7 we learn that the people of Dan "dwelt in security, after the manner of the Sidonians." For the cults practiced at Dan (the ancient Laish), see R. de Vaux, *The Bible and the Ancient Near East*, trans. D. McHugh from the French (New York: Doubleday, 1971), p. 104. The political history of this region in the second millennium B.C. has been treated by A. Malamat in "Northern Canaan and the Mari Texts," *Near Eastern Archaeology in the Twentieth Century*, ed. J. A. Sanders (New York: Doubleday, 1970), pp. 164–177.

Cyprus.[17] These sites, recently excavated, show Phoenician remains which are likely to be dated to the tenth and ninth centuries B.C.

Very little is known today about the history of Tyre and Sidon during the ninth and eighth centuries B.C. The two cities must have formed a political unity, as can be inferred from Assyrian and biblical records. For some time after 876 B.C. the Assyrians exacted tribute from all the coastal cities, including Byblos and Aradus.[18] The Assyrians needed the Mediterranean ports, and this largely explains their military incursions into Phoenician territory. The Phoenician cities failed to form a confederacy, consequently they could be used either by Assyria or by Egypt for political or commercial reasons. The preeminence among the cities of Tyre and Sidon is manifest in the fact that only the two of them were invited to the festivities organized by Ashurnasirpal II (883–859) to celebrate the inauguration of the new royal palace at Calah, the Assyrian capital. In the battle of Qarqar of 853 B.C. Tyre and Sidon did not side with the Aramaean coalition formed against Shalmaneser III, whereas Arad was listed among the participants. Tyre's, and very likely Sidon's, major enterprises overseas must have given the two cities a new political dimension in the Near East during the eighth century B.C. In 701 B.C., during the reign of Sennacherib (704–681 B.C.), Luli, king of Sidon, revolted against the Assyrians, but the Assyrian monarch marched against him and annihilated the city. In the Neo-Babylonian period which followed the fall of Nineveh in 612 B.C., Nebuchadnezzar II besieged Tyre and finally conquered it in 574 B.C.[19]

[17] V. Karageorghis, "Fouilles de Kition," *Académie des Inscriptions et Belles-Lettres, Comptes rendus des séances de l'année 1969*, 515–522, and *Bulletin de correspondance hellénique* 94 (1970), 251–258, and 95 (1971), 379–386.

[18] *ANET*, p. 276: Ashurnasirpal II's expedition to Carchemish and the Lebanon (trans. A. Leo Oppenheim).

[19] For Sennacherib's campaigns, see *ANET*, p. 288. Luli (Elulaios) is called king of Tyre by Menander in Josephus *Jewish Antiquities* (here-

The Persians became the rulers of the Near Eastern lands after they had conquered Babylon in 538 B.C. Under their administration Phoenicia, Syria, and Cyprus formed the fifth satrapy of the empire. At this time the naval power of the Phoenician cities expanded to such an extent that the ships of Sidon were considered the finest of the Achaemenid fleet, and the Phoenicians distinguished themselves in the wars of Persia against Greece.[20] The Eshmun'azar dynasty ruled Sidon from the second quarter of the fifth century B.C.,[21] when the city inaugurated her coinage.[22] Coins and inscriptions furnish important information about the history of the city; the former in particular "show that Sidon was regarded as the headquarters in Phoenicia of the Persian government."[23] In the course of the fourth century B.C. the relations between Athens and Sidon were particularly close,[24] and the Persian occupation did not prevent the Phoenician cities from becoming increasingly influenced by Greek culture.[25]

Even though information concerning Tyre is rather meager at present, it may be said that the city recovered rapidly from the defeat suffered in 574 B.C., for Herodotus mentions

---

after *J. Ant.*) 9. 283. Tyre and Sidon formed a dual monarchy at this time, but with the revolt of Luli the confederation of the Phoenician cities was disrupted and some cities, Sidon, for instance, broke away from Tyre. Josephus even says that "many cities . . . surrendered to the king of Assyria" and furnished him "with sixty ships and eight hundred oarsmen" to help him besiege Tyre; see *J. Ant.* 9. 284–285. For the interpretation of the sources dealing with the conquest of Tyre, see S. Moscati, *The World of the Phoenicians*, trans. A. Hamilton from the Italian, History of Civilization Series (New York: Praeger, 1968), p. 21.

[20] Herodotus, Book 6.

[21] J. B. Peckham, *The Development of the Late Phoenician Scripts*, Harvard Semitic Series, XX (Cambridge, Mass.: Harvard University Press, 1968), pp. 75–87.

[22] G. F. Hill, *A Catalogue of the Greek Coins in the British Museum: Phoenicia* (hereafter *BMC: Phoenicia*) (London, 1910), pp. xcii–xciii.

[23] Ibid., p. c.   [24] Ibid., p. cii.

[25] M. Smith, *Palestinian Parties and Politics That Shaped the Old Testament* (New York: Columbia University Press, 1971), p. 76.

Matten son of Siromos as the commander of a Tyrian fleet which was second only to that of Sidon.[26] Tyre resisted Alexander in 332 B.C., but the city lost her independence and received a Greek garrison.[27]

Greek and Roman writers saw the Phoenicians as a homogeneous and clever race distinct from the people of the hinterland.[28] The modern historian cannot but agree with their judgment. The study of the religious monuments left behind by the Phoenicians reveals a pantheon distinct from those of other ancient Near Eastern peoples. In the following pages we will be particularly concerned with the chief god of the Phoenicians, Baal Shamin, whose cult gained acceptance beyond his native place to become assimilated at times with the cult of the Aramaean supreme god. In Phoenicia the cult of Baal Shamin was always consistent, albeit often masked under other names. In it can be seen an intuitive approach toward monotheism unknown to Nabataeans and Palmyrenes, the two desert groups with whom the Phoenicians were in frequent contact.

BAAL SHAMIN, THE CHIEF GOD OF THE PHOENICIANS

The epithet *ba'al shamîm*, "Lord of Heaven," is used in ancient Near Eastern inscriptions as a divine name and usually denotes the supreme god of any local pantheon. Baal Shamin is already mentioned in the first part of the fourteenth century B.C. in the treaties concluded between Shuppiluliuma, king of the Hittites, and Niqmadu II, king of Ugarit.[29] Next, the name appears four centuries later in

[26] Herodotus 7. 98 and 8. 67.

[27] Arrian *Anabasis* 2. 15. 6 to 2. 24. 6. See Hill, *BMC: Phoenicia*, p. cxxiv.

[28] D. Harden, *The Phoenicians*, 2nd ed. (New York: Praeger, 1963), pp. 19–24. See also the remarks of A.H.M. Jones, *The Cities of the Eastern Roman Provinces*, 2nd ed. (Oxford: Clarendon Press, 1971), pp. 234–235.

[29] J. Nougayrol, *Le Palais royal d'Ugarit*, IV: *Textes accadiens des Archives Sud* (*Archives internationales*), Mission de Ras Shamra, IX

the Phoenician inscription of Yeḥimilk, king of Byblos, which records the dedication of a new temple: "A house built by Yeḥimilk," we read, "who also has restored the ruins of the temples here. May the Lord of Heaven and the Lady of Byblos, and the assembly of the Holy Gods of Byblos prolong the days and the years of Yeḥimilk in Byblos, for he is a righteous king and an upright king before the Holy Gods of Byblos."[30]

The title "Lord of Heaven" is to be understood as signifying the god to whom the heavens belong. Baal Shamin is thus neither the Moon god nor the Sun god,[31] but rather the equivalent of the Greek Zeus Olympios or the Roman Jupiter. He is styled the "Most High" (hypsistos), an epithet which was translated into Latin as *summus exsuperantissimus*[32] in order to indicate that he was superior to all other divine beings. Baal Shamin presided over the assembly of the Holy Ones. At Karatepe, for example, he heads a list of deities described as "the whole group of the children of the gods."[33]

Josephus, writing about A.D. 100 but quoting from reliable sources preserved in the archives of Tyre, asserts that the cult of Baal Shamin was current in that city in the age of Solomon, in the tenth century B.C.[34] By that time Tyre

---

(Paris: Imprimerie Nationale, 1956), p. 43 (RS.17.227, 51) and p. 51 (R.S. 17.340, 17). In a later decree issued by Mursilis II for the sake of Niqmapa, the second son of Niqmadu, the past treaties were ratified, and the name of the Lord of Heaven was also invoked as a witness; see ibid., p. 65 (RS.17.237, 11).

[30] *ANET*, p. 499; *KAI* 4.

[31] An Aramaic inscription from about the fifth century B.C., found in Cilicia in 1905, invokes Baal Shamin, "the great," the Moon god *šhr*, and the Sun god *šamaš*; see *KAI* 259.

[32] F. Cumont, *Les religions orientales dans le paganisme romain*, 4th ed. (Paris: Paul Guethner, 1929), p. 119. See also D. Sourdel, *Les cultes du Hauran à l'époque romaine* (Paris: Paul Geuthner, 1952), p. 30.

[33] *ANET*, p. 500; *KAI* 26: sect. III, 18–19.

[34] Josephus, of course, calls the god Zeus Olympios; see his *J. Ant.* 8. 144–148 (*Contra Apionem* 1, 118). The sources used by the Jewish historian also record the cults of Astarte and Heracles.

had certainly imposed her political supremacy on the littoral to such an extent that the cult of her god must have acquired general acceptance as a cosmopolitan deity. A reference to this theological development may, indeed, be detected in the words attributed to the Israelite king in dedicating the temple of Jerusalem: "But will God indeed dwell on the earth? Behold, heaven and the highest heaven cannot contain thee; how much less this house which I have built," and later on in the text: "when he [the non-Israelite] comes and prays toward this house, hear thou in heaven thy dwelling place" (1 Kings 8:27, 42–43).[35] The supreme god had his residence in the most elevated region of the world, above the planets and the stars; this notion was later articulated by the clergy of astronomers of Greco-Roman times, leading to the concept of a divine eternity. Thus, Baal Shamin was not only *Caelus*, i.e., the sky, or the vault of heaven, but also *Caelus Aeternus*.[36] At the beginning of the second century of our era Baal Shamin is styled "Lord of Eternity" (*mr' 'lm'*) among the Palmyrenes. It is worth noting that in a bilingual inscription from eṭ-Ṭayyibe, near Palmyra, the title *mr' 'lm'* is translated into Greek as *Zeus megystos keraunios*.[37] The expression "the Bearer of Thunder" certainly preserves the traditional character of Baal Shamin as a god of rain and vegetation, while the Palmyrenes, by using the epithet *mr' 'lm'*, seem to acknowledge Baal Shamin as a supreme god and this whether the translation of the Semitic title is "Lord of Eternity" or "Lord of the World." The title by itself indicates a further development in the theology of Baal Shamin, who during the first millennium B.C. had been conceived as a weather god only. The process initiated during Greco-Roman times went forward, for in a

---

[35] B. Mazar, "The Philistines and the Rise of Israel and Tyre," in *Proceedings of the Israel Academy of Sciences and Humanities* 1 (1967), 1–22, especially p. 20.

[36] Cumont, *Religions orientales*, pp. 118 ff.

[37] W. H. Waddington, *Inscriptions grecques et latines de la Syrie*, 2631; *CISem.*, II, 3912.

Nabataean inscription of 267 of our era *mry 'lm'* is no longer the epithet of Baal Shamin but a divine name to which a devotee addressed his invocation.[38]

Cumont remarked that the role of the Lord of Heaven changed during the last centuries of the first millennium B.C.: "When the progress of astronomy," he says, "removed the constellations to incommensurable distances, the 'Baal of the Heavens' had to grow in majesty. Undoubtedly at the time of the Achemenides, he was connected with the Ahura-Mazda of the Persians, the ancient god of the vault of heaven, who had become the highest physical and moral power, and this connection helped to transform the old genius of thunder."[39] Baal Shamin presided over the course of the stars, and thereby he happened to be thought of as accompanied by the Sun and the Moon, which thus became his acolytes. The pantheon of Palmyra, as we will see, offers a good example of this interesting development in the theology of Baal Shamin. This conception, however, was not altogether absent from ancient Near Eastern literature. In the Epic of Gilgamesh (lines 98–100) the Mesopotamian and Syrian Hadad, the god of storm and rain, was escorted by Shullat and Hanish, who were "moving as heralds over hill and plain."[40]

Evidence of the popular acceptance of the cult of the Lord of Heaven in Phoenicia is afforded by a document of exceptional interest, the treaty made by the Assyrian king Esarhaddon with Baal, king of Tyre, in 677 B.C. This was the year in which Esarhaddon captured the Phoenician city. By that time the Assyrians had succeeded in stabilizing their political relations with their western vassals and imposing

[38] A. J. Jaussen and R. Savignac, *Mission archéologique en Arabie*, I (Paris: E. Leroux, 1909), pp. 172–173, no. 17, 7.

[39] Cumont, *Religions orientales*, p. 118.

[40] *ANET*, p. 94.

what has aptly been described as a *Pax Assyriaca*.[41] The Assyrian *Chronicle* tells how the king of Tyre "bowed down and implored" Esarhaddon as "his lord," paying him a heavy tribute. The Assyrian king boasts that "he [Baal] kissed my feet. I took away from him those of his towns which are situated on the mainland and reorganized the region, turning it over to Assyria."[42] After the defeat came the treaty. Here is the text of column IV as translated by E. Reiner; it contains the curses called down on the Tyrians if they do not abide by the terms agreed on:

"May Ninlil, who resides in Nineveh, 'tie to you' a swift dagger. May Ishtar, who resides in Arbela, not grant you mercy and forgiveness. May Gula, the great physician, put illness and weariness in your hearts, an unhealing sore in your body, bathe in your own blood as if in water. May the Seven gods, the warrior gods, cause your downfall with their fierce weapons. May Bethel and Anat-Bethel deliver you to a man-eating lion. May the great gods of heaven and earth, the gods of Assyria, the gods of Akkad, and the gods of Ebernari curse you with an indissoluble curse. May Baal-sameme, Baal-malage, and Baal-saphon raise an evil wind against your ships, to undo their moorings, tear out their mooring pole, may a strong wave sink them in the sea, a violent tide [. . .] against you. May Melqart and Eshmun deliver your land to destruction, your people to be deported; from your land [. . .]. May they make disappear food for your mouth, clothes for your body, oil for your ointment. May Astarte break your bow in the thick of battle, and have you crouch at the feet of your enemy, may a foreign enemy divide your belongings."[43]

This passage clearly divides into two sections: in the first,

[41] W. W. Hallo, "From Qarqar to Carchemish: Assyria and Israel in the Light of New Discoveries," *Biblical Archaeologist*, no. XXIII (May 1960), 33–61.

[42] *ANET*, p. 291.

[43] *The Ancient Near East: Supplementary Texts and Pictures Relating to the Old Testament*, ed. James B. Pritchard (Princeton: Princeton University Press, 1969), p. 534.

Esarhaddon invokes the gods on whom he and his people relied, the "great gods" of Mesopotamia. Moreover, he calls upon Bethel and Anat-Bethel, two gods who cannot be considered native to that land. The treaty is the earliest evidence for their cult that we as yet possess. By the end of the seventh century B.C. the name Bethel appears in the theophorous names. An Aramaic tablet of 570 B.C. from Aleppo has three theophores of the god Bethel.[44] This deity is mentioned in Jeremiah 48:13, where he seems to be a god who enjoyed the confidence of certain Israelites. The personal name Bethelsharezer ("May Bethel protect the king!") of Zechariah 7:2 is to be related to the same divinity. Bethel is listed with El, Dagon, and Atlas in the pantheon sketched by Sanchuniaton in the work of Philo of Byblos.[45] The origin of his cult, however, is as yet unknown. He achieved popularity during the Neo-Babylonian period. Later on, the Elephantine and Hermoupolis papyri offer abundant testimony in favor of his cult among the eclectic society of fifth-century Egypt. Moreover, Bethel forms the name of other no less popular deities: Eshembethel ("Name of Bethel") and Herembethel ("Sanctuary of Bethel"). The element *herem* is to be linked with Arabic *haram* and means "sacred precinct." The temple thus is deified and made a new hypostasis of Bethel.[46]

Recent attempts to consider the two gods as Phoenician seem to me to be unsound. The whole structure of the treaty shows clearly that in the Assyrian chancery Bethel and Anat-Bethel were not regarded as Phoenician gods. It would be more logical to see them as of Aramaean or Syrian origin and to reject any facile association of Anat-Bethel with the goddess Anat of Ugarit.[47]

---

[44] J. Starcky, *Syria* 37 (1960), 99–115.

[45] Eusebius *Praeparatio evangelica* (hereafter Euseb. *Praep. evang.*) 1. 10. 16. The god *Baitylos* differs from the *baitylia* made by *Ouranos*; cf. ibid. 1. 10. 23.

[46] W. F. Albright, *Archaeology and the Religion of Israel*, 5th ed. (New York: Doubleday, Anchor Books, 1969), pp. 164–168.

[47] Ibid., p. 192, note 14, and J. T. Milik, *Biblica* 48 (1967), 566–567.

The second part of the document begins with the mention of Baal Shamin. Esarhaddon calls upon the gods of his vassal and implores them to punish the king if he commits treachery. A curse is called down on the area in which divine protection would be most needed by his city, namely, on the sea. Tyre, the founder of Carthage, was a maritime power. According to the Assyrian document, Baal Shamin was responsible for storms, a patron of the sea and, thus, of shipping. In the same way, the Israelite Lord of Heaven is described in the book of Jonah (1:9) as the god who creates winds and tempests.[48]

Baal Shamin seems to be equated, if not identified, with Baal Malage and Baal Saphon. The former name is still a puzzle. The latter, on the other hand, is a well-attested deity whose dwelling was in the mountain called Ṣaphân ("North") in the Ugaritic texts and Casius in Hellenistic times—the modern Jebel el-Aqra, which lies on the northern shore of Phoenicia and "served mariners as a beacon."[49] He was thus, very naturally, a patron deity of sailors, and the treaty certainly invokes him as such. Philo of Byblos mentions him first in a list of four mountain gods: Baal Saphon, Baal of Mount Lebanon, Baal of Anti-Lebanon (the Baal Hermon of the biblical texts), and Baal Brathy (evidently the Baal of the Amanus mountain).[50] The list is, of course, compounded out of ancient traditions and is therefore of

[48] Mazar, as cited in note 35 above, p. 20.

[49] W. F. Albright, "Baal-Zephon," in *Festschrift für Alfred Bertholet* (Tübingen: Mohr, 1950), pp. 1–14. Baal Saphon's character as "patron of sailors" is emphasized by an Egyptian papyrus of the XIX Dynasty. This document lists the god "Boat of Baal Saphon" among the Syrian gods of Memphis; see R. Stadelmann, *Syrisch-palästinensische Gottheiten in Ägypten* (Leiden: E. J. Brill, 1967), p. 36. See also W. Helck, "Ein Indiz früher handelsfahrten syrischer Kaufleute," in *Ugarit-Forschungen* 2 (1970), 35–37. The name *Casius* derives from the Akkadian Ḫazi (in Hittite Ḫazzi). This was the former appellation of the mountain before the North Canaanite population called it *spn* (Ugaritic ṣaphân; Phoenician ṣaphon).

[50] Euseb. *Praep. evang.* 1. 10. 9. See also Peckham, *Late Phoenician Scripts* (cited in note 21 above), p. 14, note 6.

uncertain historical value; indeed, the disarray in which these mountain gods are mentioned is in itself suspicious.

The invocation of mountain gods to ensure the inviolability of a treaty is something that was certainly not introduced by Esarhaddon but conforms to far older usage, for in a treaty between Mursilis and the king of the Amorites about 1350 B.C., the Lords of Mount Casius, Mount Lebanon, and Mount Hermon (*Sariyana* in the text) are similarly invoked.[51] The cult of such gods was carefully preserved from age to age, and constituted at all times an important element in the religious life of a nation. Alike in the ancient Mesopotamian literature and in the Canaanite poems of Ugarit, the mountain appears as the dwelling place of the gods, to whom sacrifices are offered. Readers of the Old Testament will at once recall the sacrifice on Mount Carmel in the time of the prophet Elijah. In the same way, too, Byzantine sources relate that Seleucus, after defeating Antigonus at the battle of Ipsus in 301 B.C., founded Seleucia Pieria as his new capital on the site indicated by Zeus Casius. The divine choice came after a sacrifice had been offered on top of the mountain.[52] Here, too, we are told, Hadrian sacrificed to the god in A.D. 129. The author of the *Historia Augusta* adds the interesting detail that the emperor ascended to Mount Casius by night in order to see the sunrise. Ammianus Marcellinus likewise describes a sacrifice offered by Julian in A.D. 363 and informs us that Julian "ascended

[51] *ANET*, p. 205.

[52] The story of the foundation of Seleucia is carefully recorded in the *Chronicle* written in the sixth century of our era by Malalas; see G. Downey, *A History of Antioch in Syria* (Princeton: Princeton University Press, 1961), pp. 67 ff. According to Malalas, the sacrifice took place on April 23. This can hardly be accidental as J. C. de Moor has noticed in "Studies in the New Alphabetic Texts from Ras Shamra," *Ugarit-Forschungen* 2 (1970), 306. De Moor points out that the "sacrifice of Sapanu" heads a list of offerings for the gods found at Ugarit (see *Ugaritica*, v, Mission de Ras Shamra, ed. C.F.A. Schaffer, xvi [Paris: Paul Geuthner, 1968], pp. 580 ff.: RS.24.643) and that the sacrifice must have taken place in the spring because the reverse of the tablet is headed by the month name Hiari (April/May).

Mount Casius, a wooded hill rising on high with a rounded contour from which at the second cock-crow the sun is first seen to rise" (22. 14. 4).

The Holy Family

The mention, in Esarhaddon's treaty, of the two Tyrian gods Melqart and Astarte takes us into a new aspect of the cult of the Lord of Heaven. Baal Shamin is worshiped, at Tyre and elsewhere in Phoenicia, as the chief god of a family triad, which was formed by him, his consort, and a youthful god.

The cult of Melqart, who was the Tyrian equivalent of Heracles, spread to Cyprus, Egypt, Carthage, and other places.[53] His counterpart at Sidon was Eshmun, explicitly identified with Aesculapius in an inscription of the second century B.C. from Sardinia.[54] The Phoenicians may have admitted some theological connections between his cult and that of Melqart because an inscription of the fourth century B.C. from Cyprus seems to combine Eshmun's attributes with those of Melqart.[55]

[53] G. A. Cooke, *A Text-Book of North-Semitic Inscriptions* (Oxford: Clarendon Press, 1903), p. 74; *KAI* 43, 47, 86, 201. The cult of Heracles was also popular in the Decapolis, as shown in the coins of various sites; see H. Seyrig, *Syria* 36 (1959), 62, note 1.

[54] Cooke, *North-Semitic Inscriptions*, no. 40. Eshmun seems to have been the only healer god in Phoenicia. Šadrafa, who is often considered another healer god of Canaanite if not of Egyptian origin, was most probably a deity that came into the Near East from a Persian milieu. This is now proved by the stele found at Xanthus (Lycia) bearing an inscription in Greek, Lycian, and Aramaic (*Académie des Inscriptions et Belles-Lettres. Comptes rendus des séances de l'année 1974*, pp. 82–93, 115–125, 132–149). In the Aramaic section ḥštrpty (line 25), from which the name Šadrafa must derive, is equated with Apollo. The title of "Lord of the whole World" given to Šadrafa in the Greek inscription of Maad in Lebanon (J. Starcky, *Syria* 26 [1949] 68–69) and the animals (snakes, scorpions, lions) with which he is associated at Amrit and Palmyra clearly indicate that Šadrafa was a forerunner of Mithra in the Near East.

[55] Ibid., p. 37.

Of the youth god Melqart we know that Eudoxus of Cnidos (ca. 355 B.C.) is quoted by Athenaeus (392d) as saying that the Phoenicians "sacrificed quails to Heracles, because Heracles, the son of Asteria and Zeus, went into Libya and was killed by Typhon." Seyrig has studied this text and reached the conclusion that the gods in question really refer to the pantheon of Tyre, where an original holy triad of Baal Shamin, Astarte, and Melqart became the Hellenized family of Zeus, Asteria, and Heracles.[56] According to Athenaeus, the episode of Heracles' death did not end there, for Iolaus "brought a quail to him, and having put it close to him, he smelt it and came to life again." The quail sacrifice thus would commemorate the death and resurrection of Heracles. This event was probably celebrated in an annual festival at Tyre to which Josephus seems to refer in his *Jewish Antiquities* (8. 146).[57]

Another youthful god of Phoenician mythology is Adonis, but his name—a Grecized derivation from *adonai*, "my lord"—does not appear in the inscriptions. The literary sources refer to the importance of his cult at Berytus and at Aphaca, the nearby spring.[58]

In the Phoenician inscriptions, whether written in Semitic or in Greek, these youthful gods are not associated with their parents, and their cult does not compare with

[56] H. Seyrig, "Les grands dieux de Tyr à l'époque grecque et romaine," in *Syria* 40 (1963), 19–20.

[57] A Greek inscription from Amman published by F. Abel in *Revue biblique* 5 (1908), 569–578, refers very likely to the liturgical celebration of the death and resurrection of Melqart-Heracles; see also É. Lipiński, "La fête de l'ensevelissement et de la résurrection de Melqart," in *Actes de la XVIIᵉ Rencontre Assyriologique Internationale, Bruxelles, 30 juin–4 juillet 1969* (Publications du comité belge de recherches historiques, épigraphiques et archéologiques en Mésopotamie, 1: Université Libre de Bruxelles, 1970), 30–58, but I depart in many points from Lipiński's main thesis; see my BES 1969, no. 13 and 1975, nos. 40 and 127.

[58] For the temple at Aphaca, see D. Krencker and W. Zschietzschmann, *Römische Tempel in Syrien* (Berlin and Leipzig: W. de Gruyter, 1938), pp. 56–64, and Milik, *Biblica* 48 (1967), 562.

the ubiquitous cult of Astarte in the pantheons of the Levant.[59]

Astarte was the consort of Baal Shamin at Tyre, but she was also worshiped at Sidon, Byblos, Ascalon, and at Kition in Cyprus. Her cult was especially prominent at Eryx in Sicily and on the island of Malta. At Carthage she was "the mighty Astarte." An inscription of the third to the second century B.C. is addressed to her and to the famous Carthaginian goddess Tenit as the "Ladies" of the sanctuary.[60] At Carthage the cult of Astarte seems to have merged with that of Tenit since early times, while in the Near East Astarte kept her identity and was always the goddess of fertility and generation, just what Aphrodite was among the Greeks. The Mesopotamian counterpart of Astarte was Ishtar. She was never a Moon goddess, even though late syncretistic ideas presented her as such. Lucian of Samosata, for instance, identified her with Selene,[61] but Apuleius rightly puts on Lucius's lips this prayer: "Blessed Queen of Heaven, whether you are pleased to be known as Ceres . . . or whether as celestial Venus . . . or whether as Artemis . . . I beseech you, by whatever name, in whatever aspect, with whatever ceremonies you deign to be invoked, have mercy on me in my extreme distress. . . ."[62] Astarte is the natural mother of all things, "mistress of all the elements,

[59] For the divine triads, see W. W. Baudissin, *Adonis und Esmun* (Leipzig: Hinrichs, 1911), pp. 15 ff., and H. Seyrig's remarks in *Syria* 37 (1960), 247–249, and 40 (1963), 25–26.

[60] Cooke, *North-Semitic Inscriptions*, no. 45.

[61] Lucian of Samosata *De dea syria* 4. Herodian (5. 6. 3–5) reports that the Emperor Elagabalus, being the Sun, brought the Phoenician Astarte, the Moon, to Rome to marry her. Dio in his *Roman History* (80. 12. 1) calls the goddess *Carthaginian Urania*.

[62] Apuleius *Metamorphoses* 11. 2; trans. R. Graves, *The Golden Ass* (New York: Farrar, Straus and Giroux, 1951), pp. 262–263 and 264. This reference includes the quoted phrases that follow the prayer.

primordial child of time." The goddess herself, coming out of the sea and appearing to Lucius, says that she is "worshiped in many aspects, known by countless names," but she does not appear as a Moon goddess at all. Her cult is better identified with that of the star Venus. Herodotus called her Aphrodite Urania.[63] However, we do not know whether the distinction drawn by Plato between Aphrodite Urania and Aphrodite Pandemos ("Common") was universally maintained;[64] the former, at any rate, is the one which belongs to the Semitic world.

The Greeks regarded Astarte as derived from the East, and the fashion of designating her by epithets—like "Urania," "Mighty," etc.—rather than by her proper name is characteristic of the Semites. Divine epithets tend usually to become proper names, disguising the true personality of the deity. Thus it is not a surprise to discover in the inscriptions as well as in Apuleius's book that the cult of Astarte was hidden by an abundance of names and rites. Shortly before 100 B.C. an Athenian at Delos made an offering to Aphrodite, calling her "the Holy Syrian goddess."[65] Among the titles Astarte received one is of particular interest. It appears in a Phoenician inscription of the fifth century B.C. which commemorates the construction at Sidon of a temple to her. The building was erected by the king, Eshmun'azar. The royal text styles Astarte as the "Name of Baal" whereby the goddess is believed to be a personification of the divine power. The *name* of a god, in this case Baal Shamin, works and acts. Like the Israelites, who put their trust in Yahweh's name,[66] the Phoenicians were inclined to believe that they could convey upon themselves divine assistance by merely invoking Astarte, i.e., Baal Shamin's name. An epithet similar to that of "Name of Baal"

[63] Herodotus 1. 105 and 4. 59.

[64] Plato *Symposium* 181C.

[65] W. Dittenberger, *Sylloge inscriptionum graecarum*, no. 1136.

[66] J. Pedersen, *Israel: Its Life and Culture*, trans. Mrs. Aslaug Møller, I-II (London and Copenhagen: Oxford University Press, 1926), pp. 245 ff.

is "Face of Baal," which was given to Tenit by the Carthaginians. Here again the power and the glory of Baal Shamin seem to hide themselves under Astarte's personality. This Phoenician theology is to be understood in the light of various passages of the Old Testament; for instance, according to the book of Exodus, Yahweh sent an *angel* to his people. *Angel*, or *name*, or *glory* of Yahweh are here substitutes for Yahweh's face, which no one can see without dying.[67] Maybe Astarte's part in the Phoenician pantheon was not much different from that of an angel. The cult of the angels or messengers of the supreme deities, so popular in the last centuries of the first millennium B.C., was an acknowledgment that there is a divine power that rises above the individual, and the angel's task, then, was that of mediating between god and man.

By the fifth century B.C. the sphinx had become Astarte's animal, and sphinxes then made their appearance at either side of her throne. The throne was often represented supporting the stele of the goddess rather than the goddess herself. In the same way, coins from Sidon portray a chariot carrying a litter in which a globe, i.e., the baetyl of Astarte, is visible.[68] Philo of Byblos, quoting from Sanchuniaton, says that Astarte, "travelling round the world . . . found a star that had fallen from the sky, which she took up and consecrated in the holy island of Tyre."[69] This has been correctly interpreted as referring to the baetyls adored by the Phoenicians as the idols of their goddess.[70]

The cult of steles or baetyls was universally accepted in the ancient Near East. Accordingly, it is not surprising to find holy stones of various forms associated with the cult of a particular deity. To the cult of steles of Astarte or

[67] Ibid., trans. Annie Fausbøll, III–IV (Copenhagen: Branner og Korch), pp. 647–650.
[68] H. Seyrig, *Syria* 36 (1959), 48–51, and Milik, *Biblica* 48 (1967), 574.
[69] Euseb. *Praep. evang.* 1. 10. 31.
[70] E. Will, *Berytus* 10 (1950–1951), 1–12, and Milik, *Biblica* 48 (1967), 572.

Melqart we may add the cult of the baetyl of Zeus Casius frequently represented on the coins of Seleucia Pieria.[71] The examples can be multiplied.

The cult of Astarte is often associated with that of a youthful god. Josephus, for instance, found in the archives of Tyre the information that Hiram, king of the city during Solomon's time, had erected independent temples to Astarte and Heracles.[72] Similarly, Astarte and Eshmun had their own temples at Sidon. This we know from a Phoenician inscription carved on the anthropoid sarcophagus of king Eshmun'azar (ca. 465–451 B.C.) in the Louvre. The text says that the king and his mother, Amashtart, priestess of Astarte, built the temple of the goddess in Sidon-by-the-Sea and "caused Astarte of the Glorious Heavens to dwell there." And the text follows: "We are the ones who built a temple for Eshmun, the Holy Prince, at the *ydll* spring, and we caused him to dwell in the quarter of 'Glorious Heavens.' We are the ones who built temples for the gods of Sidon in Sidon-by-the-Sea, a temple for the Lord of Sidon and a temple for Astarte, Name of Baal." This inscription is to be understood in the light of a text inscribed on several building blocks of the temple of Eshmun at Bostan esh-Sheikh; these report that the domain of Sidon was formed by four boroughs, three in Sidon-by-the-Sea: "Glorious Heavens," "Land of Reshafim," and Royal Sidon, and one in Sidon's hinterland.[73] The monarchs had obviously constructed temples in the various districts of the city. The "Lord of the City" is, of course, the chief of the holy family. On a coin attributable to the decades preceding the con-

---

[71] W. Wroth, *A Catalogue of the Greek Coins in the British Museum: Galatia, . . .* (London, 1899), pp. 272, 274 f. See also H. Seyrig, *Syria* 40 (1963), 19.

[72] Josephus *Contra Ap.* 1. 118–119 (*J. Ant.* 8. 146).

[73] *ANET*, p. 505; *KAI* 14 and 15. For the inscription from Bostan esh-Sheikh, see Teixidor, BES 1969, no. 67. The museums of Beirut, Istanbul, and the Louvre possess copies of this text; they are written upon the inner faces of the blocks and, like the inscribed bricks in Assyrian buildings, were not intended to be exposed to view.

quest of the city by Alexander the Great the god is represented as a bearded figure riding a chariot followed by the king of Sidon, who marches behind the vehicle as the priest of the city god.[74]

The Cult of Baal Shamin

The cult of Baal Shamin persisted in the region of Tyre from the time of Esarhaddon's reign until the last centuries of the first millennium B.C. One of the most recent testimonies in favor of this cult is offered by a Phoenician inscription found at the site of Umm el-'Ammed, between Tyre and Acco. The text, to be dated to 132 B.C., commemorates the construction of doors and gates in Baal Shamin's temple. The donor, 'Abdelim son of Mattan, wrote: "I built this in the year 180 of the Lord of the Kings (i.e., king Seleucus Ĭ Nicator), the 143rd year of the people of Tyre, that it may be to me for a memorial and good name under the feet of my Lord Baal Shamem for ever: may he bless me!"[75]

"Memorial" (*skr* or *zkr*) is a term well attested in Northwest Semitic inscriptions. 'Abdelim asks of his god exactly what Yahweh had promised to his devotees: "an everlasting name which shall not be cut off" (Isaiah 56:5). In this sense the name is for the Semites the expression of one's soul; it is one's honor and, therefore, can easily be identified with *zekher*, "memory," as is the case in the inscription of Umm el-'Ammed.

But at Umm el-'Ammed the cult of Baal Shamin seems to have coexisted with the cult of an important local deity: Milkastart. Inscriptions have revealed that in the third century B.C. the village worshiped him and his angel Malak Milkastart. The cult of the former must have been of great

---

[74] H. Seyrig, "Divinités de Sidon," *Syria* 36 (1959), 52–56.

[75] Cooke, *North-Semitic Inscriptions*, no. 9. For the excavations carried out at Umm el-'Ammed and their results, see M. Dunand and R. Duru, *Oumm el-'Amed* (Paris: Librairie d'Amérique et d'Orient, 1962).

importance to the villagers. He is called "the god of Hammon" (this being the ancient name of the site), and to him might have been dedicated one of the two major temples uncovered by archaeologists, for at the entrance of the sacred enclosure was discovered the pedestal of a statue bearing a dedication to Milkastart (only the feet of the figure are now visible).[76] We do not know whether the offering of 'Abdelim to Baal Shamin was made in this temple or in the other, the so-called East Temple. Both temples are very similar in plan, and both buildings were badly damaged in Byzantine times.

More relevant to our subject is a study of the personality of Milkastart. Umm el-'Ammed is the only place in the Phoenician coast where this cult is attested. The name may mean *Milk/q(art)-Astarte*. An analogous combination of deities is to be found in an inscription of the eighth century B.C. from Carthage mentioning Astarte-Pygmalion.[77] Another inscription from Carthage refers to a temple known as the "temple of Ṣid-Tenit."[78] The cult of Ṣid was widespread along the Mediterranean coasts, but the true personality of the god remains obscure as yet, even though an inscription associates him with Melqart.[79] The cult of coupled deities was a favorite creation of the Phoenician pantheons. By worshiping Milkastart the people of Umm el-'Ammed might have wanted to fuse in one name their devotion to both Astarte and Melqart, the god of nearby Tyre.

If this was the case the assemblage of the two names should not be interpreted to mean that Melqart and Astarte were united as husband and wife. Melqart was the "Lord" (*b'l*) of Tyre, and as Heracles he was a prince, a leader, an *archēgetes* (*KAI* 47), but not a Zeus. The name Milkastart

[76] Dunand and Duru, p. 48. For the inscriptions at this Phoenician site, see Milik, *Dédicaces*, pp. 423–427.

[77] Teixidor, BES 1969, no. 93.   [78] *CISem.*, I, 248–249.

[79] The cult of the god Ṣid is now well attested at Antas, in Sardinia; see Teixidor, BES 1970, no. 69.

could hardly indicate that the two personalities Melqart and Astarte had merged into one. Such a theological reasoning does not exist in the Northwest Semitic inscriptions in which, whenever two deities are invoked together the use of plural nouns, or the occasional presence of the preposition *l*-, "to," in front of each divine name leaves no room for the conclusion that the faithful worshiped them as being one. Milkastart must have been an ancestral god who assumed the function of Melqart of Tyre in the region of Umm el-'Ammed.

THE CULT OF POSEIDON

The cult of a supreme god among the Phoenicians often disguises itself under Greek names or Greek costume. Thus, the people of Berytus adored Poseidon together with Astarte and Eshmun. All three gods are present on the city's coins.[80] Even though Berytus boasted that it was founded by Kronos, as Nonus says in *Dionysiaca* 41. 68, it is Poseidon mounted on a chariot drawn by sea monsters that is systematically portrayed on local coins.

Poseidon's personality in the ancient Near East is fully revealed by a bilingual inscription of the first century A.D. from Palmyra in which he is identified with *El-Creator-of-the-Earth*.[81] But Poseidon, like El of Ugarit, had his abode in the middle of the oceans, and he embraced the Earth as the waters did for the ancients; his title therefore had more the character of "Possessor" of the Earth than its Creator. In the bilingual inscription of Karatepe, a ninth-century B.C. fortress in the Taurus mountain range, the god El-Creator-of-the-Earth (*'l qn 'rṣ*) of the Phoenician text is equated in the Luwian hieroglyphs to *ᵈa-a-ś*, the name of the Babylonian god Ea whose realm was the waters that surround the earth.[82]

---

[80] Hill, *BMC: Phoenicia* (cited in note 22 above), pp. xlvii–xlviii.

[81] J. Cantineau, *Syria* 19 (1938), 78–79; *KAI*, II, p. 43.

[82] For the pantheon of Karatepe, see M. Weippert, "Elemente phö-

The identification of Poseidon with El, the chief god of the Ugaritic pantheon, shows that the Semites had acknowledged his preeminence in the Greek world where he was believed to be one of the three sons of Kronos. It was his prominent aspect of sea-god that associated him not only with El but also with Baal Saphon, the god of the holy mountain of the Canaanites. *Ṣaphon* means "north" in Phoenician and Hebrew. It is not unlikely that the term derives from the name of Mount Saphon, which lies on the northern border of Canaan. Thus Poseidon became in the Near East the Lord of the North or, better, the Lord of the Northern Winds and, like Baal Saphon, a patron of mariners. In Esarhaddon's treaty, mentioned above, Baal Saphon is characterized as the god who can blow storms against Tyre. The harbor of Berytus needed the protection of such a maritime deity.

Poseidon protected not only the city of Berytus but also her citizens abroad. At Delos, the Berytians kept alive the cult of their national god. It is known that the island had a cosmopolitan character: Athenians, Italians, and Hellenized Oriental merchants formed associations based on religious traditions and commercial interests. The inscriptions of the last centuries before our era indicate that the principal commercial relations of Delos were with Italy and the Levant rather than with Greece. The earliest mention of a group of Oriental merchants at Delos goes back to about 178 B.C. when, according to a Greek text, a statue of Heliodorus, the minister of Seleucus IV, was erected in honor of Apollo by Phoenician warehousemen and ship-

---

nikischer und kilikischer Religion in den Inschriften vom Karatepe,' *Zeitschrift der Deutschen Morgenländischen Gesellschaft*, suppl. 1: *XVII. Deutscher Orientalistentag, 1968* (Wiesbaden: Franz Steiner, 1969), pp. 191–217, especially pp. 197, 200, 203–204. E. Lipiński also deals with the equation '*l qn 'rṣ* = Ea at Karatepe in "El's Abode: Mythological Traditions Related to Mount Hermon and to the Mountains of Armenia," *Orientalia Lovaniensia Periodica* 2 (1971), 13–69; see especially pp. 65–69.

pers.[83] Merchants, shipmasters, and warehousemen formed the association of the Poseidoniastae of Berytus. The name *Poseidoniastae*, created in honor of the chief national god, was adopted in 110 or 109 B.C.[84] The association had its headquarters on the hill northwest of the Sacred Lake. In this building the members must have celebrated their religious festivities. Three of the four chapels found there were dedicated to Poseidon, Astarte (as the Tyche of the city), and Eshmun.[85]

Besides the Berytians, other ethnic groups revered Poseidon at Delos. The association of Tyrians, devoted to the cult of Heracles-Melqart, voted to crown one of its members every year at the time when the sacrifices to Poseidon took place. This practice is of particular interest because it seems to strengthen the supposition that on the Phoenician coast Poseidon inherited the worship of Baal Saphon. The people of Ascalon, too, acknowledged Poseidon's influence, for Philostratus, their wealthy banker at Delos, made an offering of two altars, one to Astarte (*Palaistine Aphrodite Urania*) and another to Poseidon "of Ascalon."[86]

In general the inscriptions lead one to understand that the Levantine colony at Delos was prominent—and religious. In 153 or 152 B.C. the Tyrian merchants sent an embassy to Athens to request permission to build a temple to Heracles.[87] The Syrians, too, were organized in guilds, and four inscriptions mention their devotion to the triad of Hadad, Atargatis, and Aesculapius.[88] It seems that religion and patriotism rather than business or trade forged the link between these expatriate merchants. A Phoenician text found in the Piraeus in 1871 seems to me to be characteristic. It deals with the proceedings of one of these religious

[83] *Inscriptiones graecae*, XI, 1113.

[84] P. Bruneau, *Recherches sur les cultes de Délos à l'époque hellénistique et à l'époque imperiale* (Paris: E. de Broccard, 1970), pp. 622–630.

[85] Ibid., p. 628.   [86] Ibid., p. 266.

[87] *Inscriptions de Délos*, 1519 (Bruneau, *Les cultes de Délos*, p. 622).

[88] *Inscriptions de Délos*, 2224, 2248, 2261, and 2264. See also Seyrig, *Syria* 37 (1960), 246, note 2.

assemblies and runs as follows: "On the fourth day of the *marzeaḥ* (i.e. festival), in the 15th year of the people of Sidon, the community of the Sidonians resolved in assembly to crown Shama'baal son of Magon, who has been president of the corporation in charge of the temple and the building of the temple court, with a golden crown of 20 drachmae sterling, because he built the court of the temple and did all the service he was charged with; that the men who are our presidents in charge of the temple write this intention upon a golden stele, and set it up in the portico of the temple before the men's eyes. . . . For this stele let them bring 20 drachmae sterling of the money of the god, the Lord of Sidon. Thereby the Sidonians shall know that the corporation knows how to requite the men who have done service before the corporation."[89]

Inscriptions like this one must have been very frequent in the Levant. Groups of citizens residing far from their own town probably bestowed honors on compatriots who distinguished themselves in keeping alive the cults and traditions of their home. The inscription from the Piraeus shows that the members of these associations had adapted themselves to Greek civilization to such an extent that, in the case of the Sidonians of the Piraeus, the resolution which they passed was recorded "in the recognized forms used in Greek inscriptions from the fifth century downwards."[90] The members seem to have been a respectable group of well-to-do citizens whose religious concerns, however bourgeois they may appear, do not convey the same impression about Near Eastern religion in Greco-Roman times that Cumont drew from his literary, but tendentious, sources. In his *Oriental Religions* Cumont points to the Syrian slaves and itinerant *galli* populating the towns of the Mediterranean to conclude that the love of lucre among the Orientals was proverbial. But all this can hardly account for Near Eastern religious life in its entirety. Citizens hon-

[89] Cooke, *North-Semitic Inscriptions,* no. 33.

[90] Ibid., p. 95.

oring their domestic gods hundreds of miles away from
their homes afford a good example of popular piety.

THE CHIEF GOD OF BYBLOS

At Byblos, where the cult of Baal Shamin was known
from the tenth century B.C.,[91] in Hellenistic times the role
of supreme god is assigned to Kronos. His figure appears
on coins of Antiochus IV (175–164 B.C.). The god is represented nude, with three pairs of wings, two pairs outspread,
and the third pair folded. Standing, the god leans on a
scepter. The type remains practically unchanged until after
the time of Augustus.[92] It is worth noting that Philo of
Byblos, quoting from Sanchuniaton, describes Kronos in the
same manner: "He [Tauthos] devised for Kronos as insignia
of royalty four eyes in front and behind . . . but two of them
quietly closed, and upon his shoulders four wings, two as
spread for flying, and two as folded. And the symbol meant
that Kronos could see when asleep, and sleep while waking;
and similarly in the case of the wings, that he flew while
at rest, and was at rest when flying. . . ."[93]

Kronos is equated by Philo with El, the supreme god of
the Canaanites. We now know that El was the head of the
Ugaritic pantheon. Even though his part in the religious
life of the city is obscure, and even though Baal seems to
have occupied the leading place in the local cult, El remained active in the pantheons of certain other places. In
Genesis 14, for instance, he is given the epithet "Most
High" and styled "maker of heaven and earth." At Karatepe, in Cilicia, a Phoenician inscription of the ninth century B.C.[94] mentions El as "the Creator of the Earth," though
the order in which the gods are listed, namely, "Baal Sha-

---

[91] See note 30 above.

[92] Hill, *BMC: Phoenicia*, pp. lxiii–lxiv.

[93] Euseb. *Praep. evang.* 1. 10. 36–37; Hill, *BMC: Phoenicia*, p. lxiv,
note 1.

[94] For the date of the inscription, see Teixidor, BES 1971, no. 98.

min, El, the Eternal Sun and the entire group of the children of the gods," gives him only the second place.

Five hundred years after Ugarit, the epithet "Creator of the Earth" at Karatepe may well have been applied exclusively to El, and this would explain why the complete expression "El, Creator of the Earth," could be used as a single divine name. The god El-Creator-of-the-Earth was adored at Leptis Magna, in Tripolitania, in the second century A.D.[95] A contemporary bilingual inscription from Palmyra equates this deity with Poseidon.[96] It is difficult to say whether El ever possessed a distinctive personality in the pantheon of Karatepe. Possibly at the time the text of Karatepe was drawn up, a name like El-Creator-of-the-Earth was nothing more than a traditional epithet of the Lord of Heaven. Philo, for his part, identifies Baal Shamin with the Sun god,[97] thereby exemplifying a theological syncretism which was indeed widespread and an early expression of which may be seen in the pantheon of Karatepe.

The Phoenician inscriptions found at Byblos fail to offer adequate information concerning the pantheon of the city. From the tenth century B.C. onward the royal inscriptions of Abibaal, Elibaal and Sipiṭbaal I, kings of Byblos between the years 930 B.C. and 880 B.C., and of Yeḥawmilk, king during the middle of the fifth century B.C. invoke exclusively the "Lady" (baalat) of Byblos. The stele of Yeḥawmilk shows the goddess seated alone, dressed as the Egyptian Hathor receiving a bowl from the king. The preeminence of her cult over that of the Lord of Byblos seems to bear an analogy with the cult of Atargatis at Hierapolis where Hadad, the Syrian weather god, did not enjoy an actual first position in the religious life of the city either, his supremacy being overshadowed on the coins as well as in the imagery of the temple by the popularity of his partner.

[95] *KAI* 129.   [96] See note 81.

[97] Euseb. *Praep. evang.* 1. 10. 7: "They considered him [the sun] the sole god, the ruler of heaven, calling him Beelsamen, which means to the Phoenicians 'ruler of heaven,' but to the Greeks 'Zeus.' . . ."

From the Greco-Roman period at Byblos so far only an altar erected by the mason Abdeshmun bears a dedication to "our Lord" and to "the image (*sml*) of Baal" (*KAI* 12); this latter epithet certainly refers to the Lady of Byblos, and is similar to the epithets "Face of Baal" and "Name of Baal" borne by Astarte elsewhere in Phoenicia.

The presence of Kronos on the coins of Byblos, as we have seen, mirrors the popular faith in a general supreme god depicted in the figure of a foreign deity. Philo's syncretism, on the other hand, is the product of attempts at rationalization of the Phoenician pantheon by theologians and historians. But we cannot say how far, if at all, this rationalization influenced popular feelings. The Greek inscriptions of Syria certainly contradict Philo's statement that Baal Shamin was equivalent to Zeus Helios. Let aside a late inscription of Deir el-Leben from the time of Emperor Constantine, no text or monument in the Hauran departs from the traditional conception of Baal Shamin as a Lord of Heaven to whom the sun and the moon are subjected (see below, p. 81).

DEITIES OF ARADUS AND ITS HINTERLAND

After his victory at Issus (333 B.C.) Alexander decided on the conquest of Phoenicia in order to destroy the Persian fleet. While he followed the coastal route—Marathus, Aradus, Byblos, and Sidon—Parmenio, one of his generals, was detached to occupy Damascus, the Persian headquarters in Syria. This is the time when Aradus enters written history: Gerostratus, king of the Aradian region, sent his son Straton to yield the territory to Alexander.[98] The archaeological relics, however, do not illustrate much of this past, nor, for that matter, are the literary sources of more help. Scattered information about the religious life of the zone comes exclusively from coins and inscriptions.[99]

[98] Arrian *Anabasis* 2. 13. 8.
[99] H. Seyrig, "Questions aradiennes," *Revue numismatique* 6 (1964), 9–50.

The coins of the pre-Alexandrine series struck at Aradus show a marine god of unknown identity. Those of the third and second centuries B.C. represent a bearded head which is very probably that of Zeus, and a rare coin of 174/173 B.C. shows Poseidon on the obverse and Zeus on the reverse.[100] More information, though still meager, can be extracted from a Greek inscription of the late Roman period found in the medieval castle.[101] This mentions a district of Aradus named for Zeus Kronos, the god whom the faithful chose to invoke because he had manifested himself to the people more frequently than all the other gods. Theophanies were one of the well-known activities of Semitic gods. In this respect the stories of the biblical patriarchs offer an abundance of examples.

The cult of Astarte is likewise attested at Aradus both by coins and by inscriptions. The archaeological material, however, does not yet permit the reconstruction of a divine triad in that city.

On the other hand, we know that Gabala, a coastal town in the vicinity, did indeed worship such a triad, and from his frequent appearance on the Hellenistic coins found there it is certain that its youthful member was Helios (the Sun).[102] The god is rarely represented in the mintage of neighboring towns, Aradus, Carne, and Laodicea. This cult of the Sun god should not be identified, however, with that of the "Eternal Sun" at Karatepe, far less with that of the Sun at Ugarit. In the Greco-Roman period the few monuments to the Sun god erected in the Near East were dedicated by Arabs, and it is they who were responsible for the expansion of his cult.[103]

[100] Hill, *BMC: Phoenicia*, pp. xvii–xxi.

[101] See J.-P. Rey-Coquais, *Inscriptions grecques et latines de la Syrie*, VII: *Arados et régions voisines*, Bibliothèque archéologique et historique, LXXXIX (Paris: Paul Geuthner, 1970), pp. 27 ff., no. 4002.

[102] Seyrig, *Revue numismatique* 6 (1964), 22–24.

[103] The cult of the Sun is a rather popular one; see ibid., p. 23, note 1, and Seyrig's recent article "Le culte du Soleil en Syrie à l'époque romaine," *Syria* 48 (1971), 337–366.

In the Aradus region, and perhaps along the entire coast, the most famous sanctuary of all was that of Zeus at Baetocaece, in the Peraea of Aradus. The cult of this particular Lord of Heaven is known from Greek inscriptions of the Hellenistic period, but it may in fact derive from great antiquity. The records of the temple inscribed on the northern gate of the peribolos are five: one in Latin, and four in Greek.[104] They mention the prerogatives granted to the sanctuary in the last days of the Seleucid dynasty. By that time the king had become weak enough to allow the priests of the village to regain their power, and he found himself obliged to return to the sanctuary the land confiscated by the crown in order to purchase their support.

The royal order is issued in this manner: "Report having been brought to me of the power of the god Zeus of Baetocaece, it has been decided to grant him for all time the place whence the power of the god issues, the village of Baetocaece—formerly the property of Demetrius the son of Demetrius and grandson of Mnaseas [. . .] of the Apamean satrapy—with all its property and possessions according to the existing surveys and with the harvest of the present year, so that the revenue from this may be spent by the priest chosen by the god in the customary manner for the monthly sacrifices and the other things which increase the dignity of the temple, and also that there may be held each month on the fifteenth and the thirtieth day fairs free from taxation; (it has been decided further) that the temple should be inviolable and the village exempt from billeting, as no objection has been raised; that anyone who should violate any of the above provisions should be held guilty of impiety; and that copies (of this memorandum) should be inscribed on a stone stele and placed in the same temple."[105]

[104] Rey-Coquais as cited in note 101, pp. 55 ff.

[105] Translation of C. B. Welles, *Royal Correspondence in the Hellenistic Period: A Study in Greek Epigraphy* (New Haven: Yale University Press, 1934), p. 280, no. 70.

Three important privileges stem from this royal rescript:

1. The sanctuary is rendered inviolable. The Ptolemies as well as the Seleucids granted this privilege to many sanctuaries. The holy place was thereby immune from royal reprisals or private war. There were also several Syrian cities that the kings considered "holy" and "inviolable." W. W. Tarn says that "the movement was a serious attempt to limit war," but on the other hand, he recognizes that the practical effect of declaring a city holy was doubtful, "for it did not alter the political quality of a city or circumscribe its political activities."[106] The granting of asylum to a city was common in the late Seleucid monarchy. Rostovtzeff thought that this reflected the great uncertainty of life in the third and second centuries B.C. So we can say that asylum was a kind of international insurance. "By becoming 'holy' the city perhaps acquired certain privileges in respect to royal taxation; by being 'asylos' it may have been exempted from royal jurisdiction. In addition it became a place of refuge for all those, rich and poor, who were persecuted and oppressed, politically or financially, by the king and his agents. It meant for the city the influx of capital, and increase of population (that is, of military strength), and abundance of cheap labour. The grant of *asylia* may thus have been an important economic factor in the life of the Syrian cities."[107]

2. The village of Baetocaece is exempted from the burdensome duty of quartering government officials on their travels. This dispensation also relieved the populace of the necessity of providing lodgings for troops, a privilege the advantage of which can be readily appreciated.

3. Baetocaece is exempted from taxes. The religious festivals caused the arrival of quite a number of pilgrims and consequently the flourishing of local markets. This must

[106] W. W. Tarn, *Hellenistic Civilisation*, 3rd ed., 1951 (Cleveland: Meridian Books, 1966), p. 83.

[107] M. Rostovtzeff, *Social and Economic History of the Hellenistic World*, 3 vols. (New York: Oxford University Press, 1957 ed.), II p. 845.

have been a source of considerable revenue which the king was willing to renounce.

The god of Baetocaece is always named after the place itself. Worshiped as Zeus, Holy Zeus, or "the One who dwells in Heaven," one of his epithets is, as expected, *epekoos*, "the one who listens to prayers." An inscription calls him "the great Thunder god,"[108] an epithet which gives the god the indisputable status of a weather god. Written in Greek, all these epithets conceal a Semitic god whose personality appears to be that of Baal Shamin.

THE GOD OF PTOLEMAÏS

Acco, the ancient Ptolemaïs, is at the northern end of the bay of Haifa. Mount Carmel is at the other end, in the south. Under Alexander, as well as under the Egyptian ruler Ptolemy I, Acco was a fortress. The site was destroyed by Ptolemy himself when, hearing of the imminent arrival of Antigonus, he decided to flee to Egypt.[109] Ptolemy II recovered Acco, converted it into a Greek city, and gave it the name of Ptolemaïs. The coins of Ptolemy bearing the monogram of Ptolemaïs seem to have been minted after 261 B.C. In 200 B.C. the city fell into the hands of Antiochus III the Great (223–187 B.C.), who was exploiting the disturbances that followed the death of Ptolemy IV in 204 B.C. in order to regain Coele Syria and Palestine. Antiochus IV changed the city's name to *Antiochia*, but this name never became popular. We know that Herod embellished the city with a gymnasium[110] and that the Roman colony was founded between A.D. 52 and A.D. 54.[111]

---

[108] Rey-Coquais, *IGLS: Arados*, pp. 72–73, no. 4041.

[109] Diodorus Siculus 19. 93.   [110] Josephus *Jewish War* 1. 21. 11.

[111] For the history of the city, see Hill, *BMC: Phoenicia*, pp. lxxviii–lxxxii.

From Kafr Yassif, near Acco, comes a limestone tablet of the second century B.C. bearing a Greek inscription which reads as follows: "To Hadad and Atargatis, the gods who listen to prayer. Diodotus [the son] of Neoptolemos, on behalf of himself and Philista, his wife, and the children, [has dedicated] the altar in fulfillment of a vow."[112]

The personal names mentioned in the inscription are Greek, but this does not necessarily imply that the donor was Greek. Greek names—as the writer has shown elsewhere[113]—sometimes occur in bilingual inscriptions side by side with Semitic names, but the names are not translations of each other. This happens even in those cases in which a literal rendering of the Semitic name is currently used in the Greek onomastics of the period. On the other hand, the deities mentioned are indeed Semitic, as is also the content of the divine epithet *epekoos*, "the one who listens to prayer." In spite of the fact that the inscription of Ptolemaïs was written in Greek, Hadad and Atargatis have kept their identities. Only in the second century A.D., when syncretistic ideas had been widely accepted in Near Eastern society, do we find that Hadad becomes Zeus and Atargatis Hera, as, for instance, in Lucian's treatise *On the Syrian Goddess*.

Hadad, of Aramaean origin, was known as a weather god since the beginning of the second millennium B.C. This Northwest Semitic deity was among the gods of first rank for the founders of Mari, where he had a temple. Theophores of Hadad appear frequently in the documents from that city dating from the nineteenth and eighteenth centuries B.C.[114] His Akkadian name was Addu, and he was described in the Code of Hammurapi as "the lord of abun-

---

[112] See M. Avi-Yonah, "Syrian Gods at Ptolemais-Accho," *Israel Exploration Journal* 9 (1959), 1–12, especially p. 3.

[113] Teixidor, BES 1970, pp. 370–371, no. 71.

[114] H. B. Huffmon, *Amorite Personal Names in the Mari Texts* (Baltimore: Johns Hopkins University Press, 1965), p. 156.

dance, the irrigator of heaven and earth."[115] In the preface to the Code, Hadad's quality of being "propitious" is acknowledged. In the Ugaritic texts Baal is called *Hadd* and identified with the storm god; the cult of Hadad throve in Damascus during the ninth and eighth centuries B.C.[116] Josephus tells us that Hadad was the god of that city,[117] and this corroborates information gleaned from inscriptions and biblical texts. The theophorous names Ben-Hadad and Bar-Hadad, for example, are very frequent among the Aramaean monarchs of Aram and Damascus, while in 2 Kings 16:10 ff. we read that, when Ahaz visited Damascus in order to meet Tiglathpileser III, he admired the altar of the god so much that he ordered Uriah to construct a similar one in Jerusalem. The reputation of the god of Damascus lasted for centuries. When the Syrian deities became known in the Occident, Jupiter Damascenus was among those whose names were invoked most frequently in the inscriptions.

In an Aramaic inscription found at Zinjirli in 1888[118] Panamu, a king of Ya'udi in the eighth century B.C., praises Hadad, El, the dynastic god Rakib-El (the Moon god), and the Sun god for having made him king, but in the course of the text it becomes clear that it was Hadad who held the position of preeminence in the pantheon. His cult was spread through the whole of Syria. In Greco-Roman times, however, his identity is concealed under different names. At Baalbek, for example, he becomes Jupiter Heliopolitanus, while behind the epithet *Keraunios*—applied to Baal Shamin at eṭ-Ṭayyibe, near Palmyra, and in the Hauran—cer-

---

[115] *ANET*, p. 179: epilogue, reverse, xxvii, 60–70.

[116] Mazar as cited in note 12 above.

[117] Josephus *J. Ant.* 9. 93. Here the Jewish historian gives extrabiblical information; see S. A. Cook, *The Religion of Ancient Palestine in the Light of Archaeology*, Schweich Lectures, 1925 (London: Oxford University Press for the British Academy, 1930), pp. 130 ff. The temple of Hadad is probably under the Omayyad Mosque; see R. Dussaud, *Syria* 3 (1922), 219–221.

[118] *KAI* 214.

tainly lies one of Hadad's most outstanding prerogatives, that of being "the Thunderer." Similarly, at Bostra, a member of the III Cyrenaic legion dedicated an altar to him as Zeus Kyrios together with his consort, Hera.[119] The cult of Hadad and Atargatis reached Egypt in the third century B.C. At Delos some hundred years later the cult of these Syrian deities was famous, owing to the traffic in Syrian slaves which, as is well known, played an important part in the commercial life of the island. Indeed, to quote Strabo (14. 5. 2; tr. Jones, Loeb. VI, 329), Delos "could both admit and send away ten thousand slaves on the same day."

Nowhere, however, did the cult of this divine couple prevail more than at Hierapolis (Bambyce, Membidj). According to Lucian, statues of Hadad and Atargatis were carried in procession to the sea twice a year, a practice paralleled in many other ancient centers of worship.[120] People came to Hierapolis from Syria, Arabia, and even beyond the Euphrates. Although Lucian's account suggests that Atargatis in this particular center was far more important than her consort, it should not be concluded that this was the rule everywhere; it may have been simply a feature of the local cult in much the same way that local idolatrous cults of the Virgin Mary do not necessarily bespeak the attitude of the Catholic faith as a whole.

At Ptolemaïs, the cult of Hadad was at all times predominant, even when Lucian was writing about the sanctuary at Hierapolis. This is attested by a Greek inscription of the late second century or the beginning of the third century A.D., found at Mount Carmel.[121] It is inscribed on the base of a fragment of marble representing the toes and the fore-

---

[119] Sourdel, *Les cultes du Hauran* (cited in note 32 above), p. 25, where the references are given. For the inscription from eṭ-Ṭayyibe, see note 37 above.

[120] Lucian *De dea syria* chs. 33 and 47–49. H. Seyrig has made a brilliant analysis of the text of Lucian in "Les dieux de Hiérapolis," *Syria* 37 (1960), 233–251.

[121] M. Avi-Yonah, *Israel Exploration Journal* 2 (1952), 118–124.

part of a huge right foot. The object in question is certainly an ex-voto and most probably a standard type of ex-voto, for coins of Ptolemaïs minted during the reigns of Valerian (253–260) and Gallienus (253–268) portray a foot topped by a thunderbolt and with a caduceus in the right field.[122] On a coin of Antoninus Pius (138–161) found at Alexandria, the foot is surmounted by the head of Serapis, and a coin of Alexander Severus from Aegeae in Cilicia also shows a foot but with the thunderbolt atop.[123] The thunderbolt, of course, makes certain the conclusion that the ex-voto is an expression of devotion to Hadad, the weather god.

But the inscription from Mount Carmel reveals another aspect of Hadad's cult at Ptolemaïs: the donor, a colonist of the Hellenized city of Caesarea in Palestine, made his offering to *"Heliopolitan* Zeus Carmel." Let us examine the significance of the term "Heliopolitan."

The dedication of the Palestinian is made to the mountain god of Carmel at a place which had previously been the scene of a singular biblical episode. Ahab, Omri's successor to the throne of Israel (ca. 870 B.C.), married Jezebel, daughter of Ittobal, king of Sidon. Ahab's alliance with the Phoenicians greatly contributed to the prosperity of Israel, but the conflict between Jezebel and the prophet Elijah dominated his reign. Jezebel favored the Phoenician cults and persecuted the prophets of the god of Israel. When the drought announced by Elijah arrived, it was interpreted as a punishment for the worship of the god of the Phoenicians; and at this juncture, the editor of 1 Kings introduces the episode of the confrontation on Mount Carmel (18:17–46). The Baal of Carmel was not an obscure local deity. He was the Canaanite Baal whose power was believed to be manifest in winter, rain, thunder, and lightning—a power

---

[122] H. Seyrig has studied the pantheon of Ptolemaïs in *Syria* 39 (1962), 193–207; for the coins representing a foot, see his p. 201.

[123] The two coins mentioned were described by Hill in *BMC: Phoenicia*, p. lxxxvi.

which the devout Israelite attributed to his own Yahweh. It may, therefore, have been the destruction of the shrine of Zeus Carmel by the Yahwists that provided the basis for the tradition of this incident.

The priests requested of the Baal of Mount Carmel the performance of those acts which were characteristic of a supreme god, i.e., a weather god. Seyrig has drawn attention to the fact that the author of a treatise composed in the thirties of the fourth century B.C., and falsely attributed to a certain Skylax, calls Carmel the "holy mountain of Zeus."[124] Here Zeus could mean only the supreme god. More information about him can be gleaned from Tacitus, who tells us in *Histories* 2. 78 that the god of this eminence possessed there neither a statue nor a temple, but only an altar. To be sure, the Roman historian's statement must be understood strictly as referring only to this shrine on the Carmel, for at the time he wrote (104–109) the god had already come to be identified with Jupiter Heliopolitanus, who had a statue in the temple of Baalbek.[125] The statement is, however, an indication of an older tradition.

The assimilation of the Zeus of Ptolemaïs to the Zeus of Baalbek began at least in the first century B.C. In 55 B.C. Ptolemaïs had inaugurated a type of coinage which portrayed Zeus standing, with ears of wheat in his hand. This means that the city saw in him a lord of vegetation, even though in fact he resided in the high mountains; an analogous transformation must have taken place when the god of Baalbek became the god of the colonists inhabiting Berytus and its suburbs.[126]

The god of Baalbek (Heliopolis) was primarily a vegetation god. The Greek name *Heliopolis* probably points to the time when the Greeks had assimilated Baalbek's chief god to their Helios, and the similarity between the names

[124] Seyrig, *Syria* 39 (1962), 194.

[125] Ibid., pp. 200–201, and his recent article "Le culte du Soleil en Syrie à l'époque romaine," *Syria* 48 (1971), 345–346.

[126] Seyrig, *Syria* 39 (1962), 201, note 1.

of Syria's Heliopolis and Egypt's Heliopolis certainly stresses the fact that Baalbek was reorganized under the Egyptian monarchs. About 200 B.C. Antiochus the Great made Baalbek a Seleucid possession. Under the Romans the city enjoyed great prosperity, and all the Syrian cities seem to have contributed to the construction of the great temple of Jupiter, which later on was considered one of the world's wonders.[127]

The religious ties of Ptolemaïs with Heliopolis are further attested by the presence of the caduceus on the coins of the former. This appears from the time of Caracalla on. The caduceus is the emblem of Mercury at Baalbek, where it is used in the decoration of the monumental altar. Moreover, the eagle, Mercury's bird and his symbol as a messenger, is represented holding a caduceus in its beak in the so-called temple of Bacchus. Seyrig has advanced the theory that Mercury, at Ptolemaïs as well as at Heliopolis, could have been worshiped as a sort of mediator and his cult associated with the practice of the oracles.[128] These were well known in the region according to Suetonius (ch. 5), who mentions the Emperor Vespasian's visit to the oracle on Mount Carmel, near Ptolemaïs. Centuries earlier, the Phoenician prophets on Mount Carmel had asked for a dramatic intervention from their god. To provoke prophetic frenzy is a practice well documented among the Semites. The earliest example of such a phenomenon is recorded in the Wenamon papyrus (ca. 1100 B.C.) where the prince of Byblos performed a sacrifice to obtain an oracle and "the god seized one of his noble youths, making him frenzied."[129] Toward 800 B.C. Zakir, king of Hamath,

---

[127] This information is due to Malalas (11. 280. 12–14), who wrote in the first half of the sixth century. For Books 9–12, see A. Schenk von Stauffenberg, *Die römische Kaisergeschichte bei Malalas: Griechischer Text der Bücher IX–XII und Untersuchungen* (Stuttgart: Kohlhammer, 1931).

[128] Seyrig, *Syria* 39 (1962), 204–205.

[129] *ANET*, p. 26.

acknowledged the help received from the Lord of Heaven, who encouraged him to victory "through seers and diviners."[130] In their time Lucian[131] and Apuleius[132] were still able to criticize the frenzied priests of Astarte, and, for his part, Cumont has pointed out several instances of ecstasy in the cults of Asia Minor.[133] Macrobius, who wrote in the early fifth century A.D., seems to support this evidence by emphasizing the importance of divination in the temple of Baalbek and by noting how "principal persons" were "violently hurried on, not by their choice, but by the impulse of the divinity, in the same manner as the statues of the two Fortunes at Antium are carried to give oracular answers."[134]

In Phoenician sanctuaries of the Greco-Roman period the presence of a god of supreme rank, accompanied by Astarte, is not unusual. The Syrian cities of Emesa, Hierapolis, Damascus, and Heliopolis also accepted this type of ancient cult. The geographical area in which the preeminence of the supreme weather god was recognized extends along the Phoenician coast and toward the interior, including important extensions of the arable territory of Syria. Actually, the area borders the Syrian Desert to the north and the west, a fact worth stressing here. It might explain the disparity existing between the Syro-Phoenician cults and those of the Arab tribes who populated the Syrian Desert and Arabia. The religious connections observed between Ptolemaïs and Baalbek were undoubtedly part of the assiduous

[130] *KAI* 202. For this text, see recent bibliography in Teixidor, BES 1971, no. 115.

[131] Lucian *De dea syria* 36.

[132] Apuleius *Metamorphoses* 8. 27; trans. Graves, *The Golden Ass*, pp. 189–191.

[133] Cumont, *Religions orientales*, pp. 50 ff.

[134] Macrobius *Saturnalia* 1. 23. 13.

exchange of products of all kinds that took place between the coast and the Beqaa, but what kind of relations did the inhabitants of the Phoenician coast maintain with the Arab tribes of the hinterland? Did their commercial exchange cause a reciprocal influence on the religious institutions of both sides? The answer to these questions will be the task of the following chapters.

MAP II
Arabia

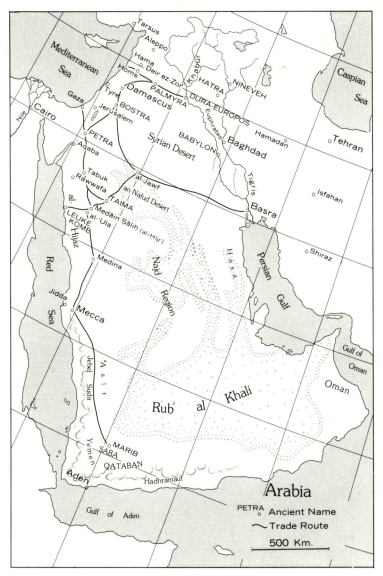

Map II. Arabia

THREE

DEITIES OF NORTH ARABIA

DURING the last four centuries of the first millennium B.C. the lands of the Near East were densely populated by Arab tribes. They had infiltrated into those areas, carrying much of their nomadic tradition. At the time of these new immigrations Hellenization was taking place in Syria, and the Phoenician cities began to be reorganized as Hellenic poleis. This simultaneous presence of two disparate cultures—Arab and Greek—blended rapidly into a new culture, to which the previous local traditions gave an adequate frame. It is understandable that the history of such a complex process should be incompletely known and that the synthesis which it produced should be revised again and again. I will try to individualize here those religious elements of Arab extraction which seem to have survived the successive political changes the Near Eastern lands went through from the fourth century B.C. to the third century A.D. at the time of Shapur's military campaign.

The Syrian Desert, a northern extension of the Arabian peninsula, forms a geographical barrier that separates the Syro-Phoenician coast from the valley of the Euphrates and the Tigris. Between the region of Damascus and the town of Deir ez-Zôr on the western bank of the Euphrates, the ridges of al-Abjaz, Abu Riǧmen, and al-Bišri cross the desert from west to northeast. A few isolated crests and numerous waterbeds, dry for the most part of the year, provide the area with water. The region, moreover, benefits from the clouds which come from the Mediterranean over the plain of Akkar in the direction of Abu Kemal. In ancient times settlements of various kinds were frequent in this northernmost part of the Syrian Desert. Sites such as Mari, Dura-Europos, Rasafa, Qasr al-Her, and Qasr ibn Wardan are well known. In recent years more archaeological sites have been discovered and excavated as a result of the rescue operation undertaken before the completion of the Euphrates Dam project.

Beyond the Euphrates, in Mesopotamia proper, the desertic lands to the east of the Khabur River were populated in the second part of the first millennium B.C. Indeed the literary tradition from Xenophon (*Anab.* 1. 5) to Dio Cassius (68. 31) treated Arabia as starting on the Khabur River. Strabo (16. 1. 27) calls these nomads very correctly *skenites*, meaning tent-dwellers. Pliny seems to have known even the names of the tribes.[1] It is interesting to note that in A.D. 121 the Parthian papyrus no. 20 from Dura-Europos mentions the existence of a *strategos* of Mesopotamia and Parapotamia who at the same time, under the title of *arabarch*, was in charge of the Arabs marauding west and south of Dura-Europos.[2] Since the whole area was predominantly inhabited by nomads, the terms "Mesopotamia" and "Parapotamia" were probably kept by the Parthians for administrative purposes only.

The southern part of the Syrian Desert is inhospitable. To the southeast of Damascus the regions of the Leja (Roman Trachonitis) and Ṣafa form a labyrinth of crackled lava. During the Greco-Roman time the area served as a "refuge" (*leja*) to the many turbulent nomads that pillaged the caravans passing through Damascus. These tribesmen wrote their names in Arabic on the glassy surfaces of ba-

---

[1] Pliny *Naturalis historia* 5. 21. 86 and 6. 29. 112. See *Syria* 43 (1966), 96–97.

[2] C. B. Welles in *The Excavations at Dura-Europos: Final Report*, v, pt. 1: *The Parchments and Papyri* (New Haven: Yale University Press, 1959), pp. 109 ff.

saltic rocks that are so characteristic of this part of the desert. The Hauran, on the contrary, is a fertile region of volcanic land which bears wheat and good pastures. The Jebel Hauran, known today as Jebel Druz because of the presence of the Druzes since the eighteenth century, separates the Leja from the plain. The Hauran, which extends to the south into the Transjordanian tableland, was the center of a continuous military and commercial activity in ancient times. It belonged successively to the Hebrew monarchy, the Aramaean kings of Damascus, and the Assyrians. Later on, with the increasing infiltration in the area of Arab tribes from the south, the Hauran acquired cultural characteristics of its own especially when the Nabataeans became the rulers of the North Arabian desert.

Further south is al-Jawf, the lower region of Wadi Sirhan; it is the biblical Dumah mentioned in Assyrian chronicles as Adumatu. A caravan route through the northwestern tip of the Nafud desert linked al-Jawf to Taima, al-'Ula (the ancient Dedan) and Madāin Ṣāliḥ. In Roman times, the Thamud occupied this commercial region of Arabia only to continue a tradition of trade that had flourished in Persian and Hellenistic times with the Minaeans and the Liḥyanites. Numerous inscriptions found in Ṣafa, the Hauran, al-Jawf, and the Dedan area attest the presence of these tribes. The texts mostly consist of the names and genealogies of their authors with occasional references to their gods. Beside the Nabataean inscriptions written in an Aramaic dialect, Minaean, Liḥyanite, Thamudic, and Ṣafaitic texts have been recorded by travelers and archaeologists. They may be dated approximately between the fifth century B.C. and the fourth century A.D. Despite their many dialectical differences the inscriptions were written in a pre-Classical Arabic. They represent the language of those tribesmen of Central and South Arabia whom either nomadism or trade had thrust northward in search of the Mediterranean markets.

ARABIAN PRIESTESSES AND DEITIES FROM ASSYRIAN TIMES

From the eighth century B.C. on, the Assyrian Annals report frequent incursions of the Arabs into Edom and Moab. The invaders were mainly the Bedouin tribes of Qedar whose rulers are called "kings of Arabia" in the Annals because they controlled the oasis of Adumatu, modern al-Jawf.[3] Qedar is associated with Taima, Dedan, and other Arabian lands by Isaiah 21:13-17 and Ezekiel 27:20-21. Even though its geographical boundaries cannot be defined, we know that the strongest opposition to Assyrian rule in North Arabia came from the region south of Wadi Sirhan. The territory must have been a principal area of settlement for the Arabs during the seventh century, and this explains why the Assyrians so often struck at it. To be sure, the Assyrians endeavored to gain control of "the great trade route leading through western Arabia from south to north towards Egypt, Damascus and the Phoenician harbor towns."[4] In their pompous Annals the Assyrian kings boasted of receiving tribute from Arab kings and queens. The queens in particular played a prominent role in North Arabian politics, as is recorded in the Assyrian Annals, which mention some five queens during these two hundred years of Assyrian domination. This, as we will see later, points to the position of the queen as a religious leader of her people.

According to the Assyrian Annals, Sargon II (721-705 B.C.) explored new areas: he went "far away, in the desert." One of the tribes mentioned in his records is that of Tamud.[5] The Tamudi are identical with the Thamudeni of the Classical texts. They had a cultic center at Rawwafa.[6]

---

[3] *ANET*, pp. 298 and 301.

[4] A. Musil, *The Northern Ḥeğâz: A Topographical Itinerary* (New York: American Geographical Society, 1926), p. 287.

[5] *ANET*, p. 286; this is also the source of the quoted phrases above and below relating to Sargon.

[6] According to a bilingual inscription (Greek and Nabataean), the

Sargon brought tribute from them and from other neigh-boring tribes "who had not yet brought tribute to any king." After his conquest, Sargon deported many of the survivors and settled them in Samaria. The system of de-portation recorded in 2 Kings 17:23–24 was fully practiced by the Assyrians at this time.

The Assyrian incursion into Arab territory continued through the reigns of Sennacherib (704–681 B.C.) and Esar-haddon (680–669 B.C.). The Annals of Esarhaddon, in fact, mention this important event: "From Adumatu, the strong-hold of the Arabs which Sennacherib, king of Assyria, my own father, had conquered and from where he has taken as booty its possessions, its images as well as the priestess queen of the Arabs, and brought (all these) to Assyria, Hazail, the king of the Arabs, came with heavy gifts to Nineveh, the town (where I exercise) my rulership, and kissed my feet. He implored me to return his images and I had mercy upon him; I repaired the damages of the images of Atarsamain, Dai, Nuhai, Ruldaiu, Abirillu (and of) Atarquruma, the gods of the Arabs, and returned them to him after having written upon them an inscription (proclaiming) the might of Assur, my lord, and my own name. I made Tarbua (or Tabua) who had grown up in the palace of my father their queen and returned her to her country together with her gods."[7] Two royal ladies are mentioned in the Assyrian sources, Tarbua and Teelhunu; the latter was the priestess-queen devoted to the service of Atarsamain. Another source records that Teelhunu became angry with Hazael, king of

temple was built during the reigns of Marcus Aurelius and Lucius Verus; see J. Teixidor, BES 1970, no. 89, and G. W. Bowersock, "A Report on Arabia Provincia," *Journal of Roman Studies* 61 (1971), 219–242, especially p. 231. The region was a Thamudaean territory; see Musil, *The Northern Ḥeǧâz*, pp. 194–195. For the inscriptions in the Tebuk area, see F. V. Winnett and W. L. Reed, *Ancient Records from North Arabia* (Toronto: University of Toronto Press, 1970), p. 56; J. T. Milik in *Bulletin of the University of London Institute of Archaeology* 10 (1970), 54–57.

[7] *ANET*, p. 291.

the Arabs, and "had him delivered into the hands of Senna-cherib." After the Arabs were defeated by the Assyrian king, Teelhunu settled in Assyria. When, later on, Esar-haddon reinstated Hazael on his throne, he, Esarhaddon, was willing to return Teelhunu to the Arab monarch in view of her position as priestess, but apparently he refused to send Tarbua back, an understandable act because she "had grown up in the palace" of the Assyrian monarch, and Esarhaddon must have had great affection for her. Probably at the request of Hazael, Esarhaddon consulted the oracle of Shamash to learn whether he had to return the princess to her country. The answer of the oracle was affirmative.[8]

The mercy shown by Esarhaddon to Hazael did not pre-vent Assurbanipal (668–633 B.C.) from punishing Uate, king of the Arabs, when he "cast away the yoke" of the Assyrian ruler. Assurbanipal accused him of refusing "to come (and) to inquire" about the royal health and of holding back "the presents and his heavy tribute." This most insubordinate behavior prompted a new military expedition of the As-syrians. The king marched through the desert "where parch-ing thirst is at home, where there are not even birds in the sky and wherein neither wild donkeys (nor) gazelles pas-ture." Assurbanipal pursued Uate and his ally, Abiate, until he defeated them. The records describe the Arabs as having formed a confederation in this faraway desert.[9] It comprised the Isamme clan, whose members were worshipers of Atar-samain, and the Nabaiati, the Nebaioth of the Old Testa-ment.[10]

---

[8] *ANET*, pp. 291–292, 299, 301. The last of these pages is the source of the quoted phrase concerning Teelhunu and Hazael.

[9] *ANET*, p. 299. For the source of the quotations describing the mis-deeds of Uate, see ibid., p. 297; for the description of Assurbanipal's march through the desert, see ibid., p. 299.

[10] Some inscriptions from the Taima area published by F. V. Win-nett in *Ancient Records from North Arabia* mention the tribe of the *Nabayat*, i.e., the Nabaiati of the Assyrian chronicles and the Nebaioth of the Old Testament. The new Arabic spelling Nebayoth prevents any possible identification of the tribe with the Nabataeans; see Winnett,

The position of preeminence granted by the Assyrian records to the Arabian queens can be accounted for by the fact that they were the priestesses of that Bedouin society. Occasionally the name of the queen is disregarded and only the title of her function as priestess is recorded.[11] This seems to indicate the existence of a strong theocratic society. A few centuries before the Christian era the priest-princes (*mukarrib*) of South Arabia also exercised their rulership in a theocratic manner. This was likewise the case with the Arab dynasts in Syria during the last three centuries B.C. At Hatra, an inscription gives the father of the first king of the town the titles "priest" and "lord"; his political status is paralleled at Tell es-Shughafiyeh in the Delta where a Nabataean inscription also calls the local ruler "priest" and "lord."[12]

In the list of the idols taken away by Sennacherib from the Arab tribes two names, Atarsamain and Ruldaiu, are of particular interest. Atarsamain's cult was widespread among the tribes of North Arabia, although it is not attested in the Nabataean inscriptions. The gender of Atarsamain (*'Attar-šamain*, "Morning Star of Heaven") is uncertain, even though the deity represented a personification of the planet Venus. Identification of Atarsamain with the Arab goddess Allat has been proposed but encounters difficulties because, under Hellenistic influence, for the Arabs Allat became identical with Athena, the Greek goddess of war. According to Herodotus (3. 8), however, for the Arabs Allat was the equivalent of Aphrodite Urania, the Phoenician Astarte. This stellar aspect of Allat is partly manifest

---

p. 31. For the cult of Atarsamain among the Arabs, see M. Weippert, "Die Kämpfe des assyrischen Königs Assurbanipal gegen die Araber," *Die Welt des Orients* 7 (1972), 44–45.

[11] R. Borger, *Orientalia* 26 (1957), 8, note 11.

[12] J. Teixidor, "Notes hatréennes," *Syria* 43 (1966), 91–93. The institutional dissociation of the two titles must have taken place at Hatra some time before the establishment of the monarchy. J. T. Milik has misunderstood me in his book *Dédicaces* . . . (Paris: Paul Geuthner, 1972), p. 361.

at Palmyra where the Arab families invoked their patron deity sometimes as Allat, sometimes as Astarte-Ishtar. At all events, it seems that the Arabs worshiped Venus, the morning star, as a warrior. Julian says plainly that the people of Edessa thought that Azizos, the male representation of Venus, was Mars.[13] What they thought in fact was that the morning star had a warrior aspect which could be regarded as the personification of Mars, the war god. Here we may have an echo of a tradition which makes the identification of Allat with Athena understandable.

The other deity of paramount importance in the Arab pantheon is Ruldaiu. He is to be identified with the god Orotalt of the Arabs, mentioned by Herodotus (3. 8). His personality has been correctly interpreted only recently.[14] Orotalt was the god Ruḍa (rḍw), but at the time of Herodotus the ḍad of Ruḍa was very likely pronounced with a lateral lamedh, thus the name could have easily been understood by a Greek as *Rodl*, which becomes *Rodal* or *Rotal*. The phenomenon is similar to what has occurred in Spanish with the Arabic word *câḍi*, which became al-*calde* ("mayor"). The initial *o* in Orotalt is certainly prothetic. The pre-Islamic Arabs of Thamud and Ṣafa profusely acknowledged the cult of Ruḍa in their inscriptions. The former group, with their vital center at Madāin Ṣāliḥ (al-Ḥijr), both antedated and survived the Nabataeans; the latter inhabited the desert region southeast of Damascus, and their language represents "the most northerly extension of the Ancient Arabic script and one of the most evolved

<hr/>

[13] Julian *Orationes* 4. 150CD. The text of Julian's oration acknowledging Iamblichos's identification of Azizos and Monimos with Ares and Hermes has been recently studied by H.J.W. Drijvers, "The Cult of Azizos and Monimos at Edessa," in *Ex Orbe religionum* [Festschrift G. Widengren] (Leiden: E. J. Brill, 1972), pp. 355–371. For an overall view on the studies dealing with the cult of Atarsamain see Weippert's article cited in n. 10.

[14] J. Starcky, "Pétra et la Nabatène," *Supplément au Dictionnaire de la Bible* (hereafter *Suppl. DB*), VII (Paris: Letouzey & Ané, 1964), col. 991.

forms of it."[15] The oldest Safaitic inscriptions date from the first century B.C. In their monuments the mention of the god Ruḍa (rḍw/rḍy) is accompanied by the figure of a danseuse, naked and holding her tresses with her hands. The importance of this cult is indirectly stressed by the rage with which al-Mustawghir destroyed the temple of the god in the early years of Islam. The incident is narrated by ibn-al-Kalbi, who puts in the mouth of this "irascible" puritan the following verses: "I marched against Ruḍa and burnt it down, and left it a heap of ashes, charred and black. I called upon 'Abdullāh's aid for its destruction; verily it is one like 'Abdullāh who would dare unlawful things to do."[16]

Orotalt, a supreme god, was believed to be Dionysus by Herodotus (3. 8). According to Strabo (16. 1. 11), the Arabs adored two gods, Dionysus and Zeus. But Origen, better informed than Strabo, follows Herodotus' opinion that the two Arabian deities are Dionysus and Urania, and he adds: "for in them the male and female sexes are glorified. . . ."[17] The identification of Orotalt with Dionysus is understandable only if the former had become a god in charge of vegetation. Dushara, the Nabataean deity, is often given the aspect of a vegetation god in regions of fertile soil like the Hauran.[18] But this type of cult definitely points to a time in which the transition from the simplicity of the desert to a certain opulence had already taken place. In the case of Dushara, his identification with Dionysus seems coherent; it is not so in the case of Orotalt. Unfortunately, Herodotus did not inform us about the daily life of the Arab tribes he knew.

15 F. V. Winnett, *Safaitic Inscriptions from Jordan* (Toronto: University of Toronto Press, 1957), p. 1.

16 Hishām ibn-al-Kalbi, *The Book of Idols*, trans. N. A. Faris (Princeton: Princeton University Press, 1952), p. 26.

17 Origen *Contra Celsum*; trans. H. Chadwick (Cambridge: At the University Press, 1965), p. 294.

18 See D. Sourdel, *Les cultes du Hauran à l'époque romaine* (Paris: Paul Geuthner, 1952), pp. 20 and 63–64; see also note 44 below.

Taima and Its Pantheon

The earliest reference to Taima, an important trade and religious center of North Arabia, is found in the Annals of Tiglathpileser III (744–727 B.C.),[19] but it is not until the years of Nabonidus (555–539 B.C.), king of Babylonia, that the city attained a prominent role in the Near East. Nabonidus lived there ten years, as we learn from the cuneiform steles found at Harran.[20] These inscriptions also inform us that Nabonidus exercised control over "a desert tract studded with oases extending some 250 miles (from Taima to Medina) and of irregular width up to about 100 miles."[21] After fighting the Arab tribes, Nabonidus made peace with them, but we do not know who they were. He settled colonies of Babylonians in these oases, as is clearly asserted by the following words from one of the Harran inscriptions: "In plenty and wealth and abundance my people in the distant tracts I spread abroad."[22]

This long sojourn of the Babylonian court at Taima must have influenced some aspects of its daily life, as the Aramaic stele found by Charles Hubert in 1880 to some extent attests. This monument should be dated on archaeological and paleographical grounds to the time of Nabonidus,[23] but how the stele is to be related to his presence in the oasis is not easy to say. The text of the inscription is partly damaged. Here is its translation:

". . . in the 22nd year . . . in Taima, Ṣalm of Maḥram and Shingala and Ashira, the gods of Taima, to Ṣalm of *hgm* . . . appointed him on this day in Taima . . . which Ṣalm-shezeb son of Petosiris set up in the temple of Ṣalm

---

[19] *ANET*, p. 283.

[20] C. J. Gadd, "The Harran Inscriptions of Nabonidus," *Anatolian Studies* 8 (1958), 35–92.

[21] Ibid., p. 84.   [22] Ibid., pp. 63–65.

[23] Recently I advocated a date at the very beginning of the fifth century B.C. (see *Journal of the American Oriental Society* 92 [1972], 530), but on stylistic grounds the stele can very well date back to the time of Nabonidus; see Winnett and Reed, *Ancient Records from North Arabia*, p. 92.

of *hgm*, therefore the gods of Taima made grants to Ṣalm-shezeb son of Petosiris and to his seed in the temple of Ṣalm of *hgm*. And any man who shall destroy this pillar, may the gods of Taima pluck out him and his seed and his name from before Taima! And this is the grant which Ṣalm of Maḥram and Shingala and Ashira, the gods of Taima, have given to Ṣalm of *hgm* . . . from the field 16 palms, and from the treasure of the king 5 palms, in all 21 palms . . . year by year. And neither gods nor men shall bring out Ṣalm-shezeb son of Petosiris from this temple, neither his seed nor his name, who are the priests in this temple for ever."[24]

The text is altogether obscure, yet various conclusions can be drawn from it. Taima was on a crossroad for the caravans going to Egypt or to Mesopotamia. Its abundant spring made the site an obligatory halt for travelers, hence its cosmopolitan character. The name of the father of the donor, for instance, is Egyptian; the reliefs on the stele show definitively the influence of Assyrian art; and the language of the stele is Aramaic, which by then had become the international language of the Near East. Unfortunately, the pantheon of Taima as it appears in the inscription eludes us. The personalities of the members of the triad remain totally unknown. More interesting is the way in which the inscription reports the introduction of the new god Ṣalm of *hgm* into the pantheon of the town as an event sanctioned by the local gods Ṣalm of Maḥram, Shingala, and Ashira. Since the chief god of Taima was Ṣalm of Maḥram and the guest god was Ṣalm of *hgm*, the word *ṣalm* must have had a precise meaning at Taima. I think that the names *Maḥram* and *hgm* stand for the cult places in which the two gods were first adored. Later on, when Taima became an important center for the region, their cults moved into the city one after the other. *Ṣalm* usually means "image," but here the translation "idol" seems more pertinent. Accordingly,

---

[24] G. A. Cooke, *A Text-Book of North-Semitic Inscriptions* (Oxford: Clarendon Press, 1903), p. 196, no. 69.

the inscription would commemorate the inclusion of the "idol" of *hgm* in the pantheon of Taima.

At this early period the Arab idols consisted most probably of stones of various forms with schematic anthropomorphic features, if any. Only foreign influences made the Arabs adopt, in place of their ancestral idols, statues as current representations of their gods. In the case of the Liḥyanites foreign elements can be detected in the archaeological remains uncovered in their capital at Dedan, modern al-'Ula, formerly a Minaean halt on the incense route.[25] The royal statues of Aswan, from the end of the first century B.C.,[26] and the statues of the Nabataeans typify the last stage of a long process which has been intelligently described by ibn-al-Kalbi in his *Book of Idols*. According to this author, one of the most prolific writers of early Islam, the son of Abraham "settled in Mecca," where "he begot many children"; later on, "Mecca became overcrowded with them, and dissension and strife arose among them, causing them to fight among themselves and consequently be dispersed throughout the land, where they roamed, seeking a livelihood. The reason which led them to the worship of images and stones was the following: No one left Mecca without carrying away with him a stone from the stones of the Sacred House as a token of reverence to it, and as a sign of deep affection to Mecca. Wherever he settled he would erect that stone and circumambulate it in the same manner he used to circumambulate the Kaabah (before his departure from Mecca). . . . In time this led them to the worship of whatever took their fancy, and caused them to forget their former worship. They exchanged the religion of Abraham and Ishmael for

[25] Anatolian, Syrian, and Egyptian influences have been detected in the architecture and the statuary of the region; see A. Grohmann, *Kulturgeschichte des Alten Orients: Arabien* (Munich: C. H. Beck, 1963), pp. 46–48 and 74–78.

[26] J. Pirenne, *Le royaume sud-arabe de Qatabân et sa datation* (Louvain: Publications Universitaire, 1961), pp. 138–140.

another. Consequently they took to the worship of images, becoming like the nations before them."[27]

From this text I conclude, first, that the Arabs before Islam, and under foreign influence, changed their original cult of stones for that of statues and, second, that by imitation of foreign statues the stone idols were given living personalities not necessarily related to what the statues stood for for non-Arab worshipers. The incongruous relationship which existed between the god and his physical appearance in stone was sarcastically put in evidence by the author of the Syriac homily of Pseudo-Meliton. The document was written in the third century A.D. The author, a fervent follower of the euhemeristic school, described the pagan cults of the Syriac-speaking communities of North Mesopotamia, most of which were Arab. In connection with Hierapolis, for instance, he says: "All the priests who are in Mabug know that Nebo is the image (ṣlm) of Orpheus, a Thracian magus, and Hadran [sic] is the image of Zoroaster, a Persian magus."[28] In other words, a Mesopotamian god, Nebo, had been identified with a Greek demigod, and Hadran, the Syrian god Hadad, had been given the personality of a Persian.

The Taima stele has been compared by C. J. Gadd with contemporary Babylonian steles found at Harran.[29] This association seems to be correct and indeed helps us to understand the Taima monument better. Gadd notes that the Harran steles represent the emblems of the Sun god, the Moon god, and Ishtar. The emblem of the Sun god, the winged disk, appears at the top of the Aramaic stele of Taima, where it hovers above a standing human figure with an extended right arm. According to Gadd, this figure would be the "image" of the god of hgm being received by the

27 Ibn-al-Kalbi, The Book of Idols, p. 4.

28 Syriac homily of Pseudo-Meliton, edited by E. Renan, in J. B. Pitra, Spicilegium Solesmense (Paris, 1885), p. xliii.

29 Gadd, Anatolian Studies 8 (1958), 42.

74

Taima gods, while the disk would stand for the "image" of the god of Maḥram.

But this interpretation does not seem likely, for bull heads are frequently found with inscriptions mentioning the god Ṣalm.[30] Rather, these bucrania would suggest that Ṣalm's cult is to be associated with that of the Moon god. The enthusiastic devotion of Nabonidus for the cult of the Moon god may partly explain the interest of the Babylonian monarch in Taima if the town was indeed a center of Moon worship. The inscriptions, however, do not specify which one of the two gods Ṣalm was venerated in the region. Ṣlm, i.e., "the idol," or "the sacred stone," embodied a numinous power that aroused awe among its worshipers. Expressions such as ṣlm of mḥrm, or ṣlm of ḥgm presumably indicated that ṣlm was believed to be the tutelary numen of a given locality. In this respect ṣlm can be very likely compared to gny', "jinn" or "supernatural protector," whose cult was profusely spread in the Palmyrene region where seminomadic tribes, attracted by the splendor of Palmyra, had settled. They practiced ancestral cults of their own. In 1933 and 1935 D. Schlumberger excavated the area northwest of Palmyra, uncovering a great number of inscriptions that were for the most part votive. They often mention the gny' as the tutelary deities of villages, settlements, encampments, orchards, tribes, etc.

Our meager information about the North Arabian cults does not permit more than hypothetical conclusions, and the pretentious lists of Arabian gods compiled by some scholars from the inscriptions so far uncovered are far from presenting a well-defined pantheon. The lack of theological thought among the Arabs who preceded the Nabataeans in North Arabia may possibly be related to the nomadic character of their lives. On the other hand, the abundance of cults and divine names described by ibn-al-Kalbi as proof of the polytheistic practices of the tribes before Islam may simply re-

[30] Winnett and Reed, *Ancient Records from North Arabia*, p. 93.

flect the worship of a unique god who was believed to manifest himself in a plurality of ways. It is not possible, though,
to say that these were true theophanies nor, for that matter,
to conclude that the North Arabian tribes had a monotheistic religion. Ibn-al-Kalbi clearly states that the Nizar, for example, a well-known group from North Arabia, had polytheistic cults, and he applies to them Sura 12. 106: "Most
of them do not believe in God without also associating other
deities with him (*mushrikun*)." Of course the belief that
there was a supreme god with whom other divine beings
who acted as "deities" were associated should exclude the
concept of an Arabian pantheon consisting of an undis-
criminated plurality of gods. In fact, according to Herodotus
and, later on, to Origen the pre-Islamic Arabs believed only
in a god and a goddess. I would surmise that in their statements Herodotus, an inquisitive traveler, and Origen, an
occasional preacher among the Arabs, intended to point out
the comprehensive notion of the divine held by the Arabs
rather than the folkloric aspect of a devotion to a pair of
male and female deities.

THE NABATAEANS: AN OUTLINE OF THEIR HISTORY

Little more than the sparse information set forth above
is at present available to anyone interested in studying the
religious institutions of the Arabs before the arrival of the
Nabataeans. With the Nabataeans the panorama changes.
The Nabataeans, originally a nomadic people, first appeared
in 312 B.C. Syria and Palestine were occupied at this time
by the forces of Antigonus, the Macedonian general who
expelled the troops of Ptolemy in 315 B.C. at the outbreak
of war between the two generals. In 312 B.C. Antigonus decided to make a campaign against the Nabataeans of Petra,
obviously as a preliminary step to the invasion of Egypt,
but the Greeks were defeated. It is worth recalling here the
comments of Diodorus of Sicily on the Nabataeans and their
land: "The Arabs who inhabit this country, being difficult

to overcome in war, remain always unenslaved; furthermore, they never at any time accept a man of another country as their overlord and continue to maintain their liberty
unimpaired. Consequently neither the Assyrians of old, nor
the kings of the Medes and Persians, nor yet those of the
Macedonians have been able to enslave them, and although
they led many great forces against them, they never brought
their attempts to a successful conclusion" (2. 48. 4–5).[31]
Diodorus also notes that the Nabataeans at this time far
surpassed the other Arabs in wealth, although they were not
much more than ten thousand in number. The same author
gives us an important detail regarding their language. In
the aftermath of the war the Nabataeans sent a letter to
Antigonus written in "Syriac" characters (19. 96). This
means that they had already abandoned their local dialect
and accepted Aramaic as their official language. In other
words, the Nabataeans accommodated themselves to their
new environment. By the end of the second century B.C.
Nabataean had become an independent language.

The beginning of Nabataean history remains obscure.[32]
We do not know, for instance, when the rulers were given
the title of king. One of the earliest inscriptions, that of
Khalasah, a site on the road from Avdat to Gaza, mentions
a certain Haretat, king of the Nabataeans. This inscription,
however, can be dated only approximately, from about 200
B.C. To be sure, when the first Ptolemies of Egypt began
to stimulate the systematic exploration of Arabia in order
to open new markets, the Nabataeans were already at the
main crossroads of the peninsula. From their kingdom in
the desert of Edom they moved northward, subduing the
land as far as Damascus. Some evidence for their commercial activity during the third century B.C. is provided by
the papyri from the archives of the Egyptian agent Zenon.

[31] I follow the translation of C. H. Oldfather, Loeb Classical Library
(Cambridge, Mass., 1961), p. 43.
[32] In these pages I shall follow the valuable article of J. Starcky,
"Pétra et la Nabatène," in *Suppl. DB*, VII, cols. 886–1017.

Aretas I is the earliest Nabataean ruler of whom we have any considerable knowledge. He is called "tyrant of the Arabs" shortly before the Maccabaean revolt (2 Macc. 5:8). Aretas held captive the high priest Jason when he was ousted from Jerusalem in 168 B.C. The title "tyrant" indicates that Nabataea was an independent principality at this time. In 163 B.C. Judas Maccabaeus carried out a series of campaigns against the countries around Judaea. By then the Nabataeans occupied territory from Moab, in the north, down to al-Ḥijr, the southern limit of their kingdom. Diodorus says that they controlled "a large part of the coast [i.e., the Red Sea coast from the Gulf of 'Aqaba to Leuce Kome, north of the present Yenbo] and not a little of the country which stretches inland" (3. 43. 4).[33]

Obodas I, son of Aretas II, defeated Alexander Jannaeus about 93 B.C. This event marks the emergence of the Nabataeans as a powerful people. In 86 B.C. Antiochus XII, the last of the Damascus Seleucids, crossed Judaea in order to attack the Nabataeans; he was defeated and slain in battle by Obodas, who thus became master of the country as far as Damascus. At his death Obodas was deified: an inscription at Petra commemorates the erection of a statue in honor of Obodas the god (*'lh'*), and a temple uncovered at Avdat seems to have been dedicated to Zeus Obodas and Aphrodite in A.D. 268.

Aretas III succeeded in controlling Coele Syria. He had been appointed to the throne of Damascus by the people of the city because they resented Ptolemy, the tetrarch of Chalcis in the Lebanon region. Aretas was king of Damascus from 84 to 72 B.C. In 72/71 B.C. the Armenian king Tigranes invaded Coele Syria, and Aretas was forced to abandon Damascus. When Lucullus, the Roman general, attacked Armenia, Tigranes withdrew from Syria. In 63 B.C. Pompey was at Damascus and created the Roman province of Syria. Meanwhile, in Jerusalem John Hyrcanus II

---

[33] Trans. Oldfather, Loeb, pp. 213–215.

had been defeated by his brother Aristobulus, who claimed for himself the high priesthood and the royal dignity. Hyrcanus went to Petra with Antipater, the father of Herod the Great, and prepared an army to attack Jerusalem. In 65 B.C. Aretas sent his troops against king Aristobulus and besieged the Temple. Pompey ordered Scaurus to march on Jerusalem. Aretas was forced to raise the siege and withdraw his army. Coins struck at Rome by Scaurus represent the Nabataean king kneeling beside his camel.[34]

Obodas II was king from about 30 to 9 B.C. The power was in the hands of his minister Syllaios, who, in 25 B.C., accompanied the prefect of Egypt, Aelius Gallus, to Arabia Felix (Yemen). Strabo (16. 4. 23) has left a detailed report of this expedition, which happened to be a failure. The event was a turning point in Nabataean history because Augustus decided, from then on, to convey the major part of the caravan trade to Egypt, which was annexed to Rome about 30 B.C. Augustus carefully recorded this event in his *Res gestae*: "I added Egypt to the dominions of the Roman people."[35] From this moment onward Nabataea declined as a political power.

Aretas IV was king of the Nabataeans from 8 B.C. to A.D. 40. He was surnamed "lover of his people" (*rḥm 'mh*), a title that asserts the king's claim to independence. Numerous Nabataean inscriptions are dated from his reign; most of the funerary inscriptions of al-Ḥijr were carved during these years—years politically disturbed by the unrest that flared up after Herod's death. In the Hauran Nabataean continued to be used, though less than Greek. The region had been attached to the kingdom of Herod in 23 B.C. According to a Nabataean inscription, a temple was dedicated by an Arab, Malikat son of Ausho, to Baal Shamin at Siʻa, the high place of the Jebel Druze. The construction lasted

[34] Starcky, *Suppl. DB*, VII, col. 909, fig. 695, 2.

[35] H. I. Bell has studied the peculiar way in which Egypt was annexed to the Roman empire; see his *Egypt from Alexander the Great to the Arab Conquest* (Oxford: Oxford University Press, 1966), pp. 65 ff.

from 33/32 B.C. to 2/1 B.C.[36] The building undertaken by Malikat comprised the following structures: the cella, the temple itself, and its portico. The last is called in Nabataean *tytr'*, a word which with great probability derives from the Greek *theatron*. According to the inscription, Malikat also paid for the roof. The whole was built within a rectangular enceinte which opened on a huge forecourt.[37] A second inscription found in the area of the temple informs us that Malikat's grandchild contributed to part of the religious compound. The tribe of the Obaishat acknowledged this by dedicating a statue to him in the portico.[38] Herod himself, who had a statue set up at the entrance of the cella, may have contributed to the construction of the sanctuary. The monarch's interest in the erection of magnificent public buildings all over his kingdom seems to support this conclusion. After his death, his son Philip, who had received Auranitis, Batanaea, Trachonitis, Gaulanitis, and Ituraea, continued the family tradition and also left behind imposing monuments. The Nabataean inscriptions give Philip the title *tetrarch,* not *king,* but the fact that they date according to his regnal years may indicate that he was a popular ruler.[39]

[36] J. Cantineau, *Le Nabatéen: Choix des textes; lexique,* II (Paris: E. Leroux, 1932), pp. 11–13. The text of the inscription is written in the architrave of a portico. For the history of the recovery of the various fragments, see E. Littmann, *Semitic Inscriptions,* Publications of an American Archaeological Expedition to Syria in 1899–1900, IV (New York: Century Co., 1904), pp. 85–90, and *Semitic Inscriptions,* sect. A: *Nabataean Inscriptions,* Publications of the Princeton University Archaeological Expeditions to Syria in 1904–1905 and 1909, div. IV (Leiden: E. J. Brill, 1914), pp. 76–78.

[37] For the plans, see H. C. Butler, *Architecture,* sect. A: *Southern Syria,* Publications of the Princeton University Archaeological Expeditions to Syria in 1904–1905 and 1909, div. II (Leiden: E. J. Brill, 1919), pp. 365–402. See also P. Collart and J. Vicari, *Le sanctuaire de Baalshamin à Palmyre: Topographie et architecture,* Bibliotheca helvetica romana, X, 2 vols. (Neuchâtel: P. Attinger, 1969), I, pp. 190–198.

[38] Cantineau, *Le Nabatéen,* II, p. 13.

[39] Ibid., pp. 15–16.

The persistency of the Nabataean language in a region which was under Jewish rule supports the conclusion that Nabataean tribes settled in the region long before the arrival of Pompey in Syria, when major changes in the administration of Syria took place. The Nabataeans had probably become acquainted with the cult of Baal Shamin during their wanderings in the Hauran. This most probably started at the beginning of the second century B.C.[40] Fervor for the Lord of Heaven must have been intense in this region of fertile soil because the inscriptions attest a great number of theophorous names of Zeus, whose cult certainly took over that of a Semitic Baal.[41] The popularity of Baal Shamin among the Nabataean-speaking tribes of the Hauran is not paralleled by a similar cult among the tribes living in the southern part of Nabataea, which is understandable since the latter were more concerned with caravan traffic than with agriculture.

The Nabataeans living in the Hauran detached themselves from their Arabian origins, transforming their life into a sedentary one to such an extent that the art they produced mirrored the new patterns of life. Agricultural motifs, for instance, borrowed from Greco-Oriental art, favored then by the Syrians,[42] were easily incorporated into the Nabataean monuments.[43] Settlement in cultivable lands prompted the Nabataeans of the Hauran to ask for help from the Phoenician Lord of Heaven. The temple they dedicated to Baal Shamin at Si'a proves that the urgency

[40] 1 Maccabees 5:25 and its parallel in 2 Maccabees 12:10-12. See Starcky, *Suppl. DB*, vii, col. 904-905.

[41] Sourdel, *Les cultes du Hauran* (cited in note 18 above), p. 20.

[42] Greco-Oriental, or Greco-Parthian, art is the object of an important study by D. Schlumberger, *L'Orient hellénisé: L'art grec et ses héritiers dans l'Asie non méditerranéene*, Collection: "L'art dans le monde" (Paris: Éditions Albin Michel, 1970).

[43] Starcky, *Suppl. DB*, vii, col. 941; see the archaeological materials collected by M. Dunand in *Le Musée de Soueïda* (Paris: Paul Geuthner, 1934), part of the *Mission archéologique au Djebel Druze* in the series Bibliothèque archéologique et historique, xx.

of the new cult was acknowledged. For Arrian, writing in the second century A.D., the supreme god of the Arabs settled in Syria was *Ouranos*, i.e., heaven personified as a god.[44]

Rabbel II, the last Nabataean king, reigned from 71 to 106. He made Bostra his second capital, where a dynastic temple seems to have existed. In the nearby Imtân an inscription commemorates the offering of an altar "to Dushara-A'ra, the god of our lord, who is at Bostra." The text is dated from the twenty-third year of Rabbel, i.e., A.D. 93.

After Rabbel's death Trajan incorporated Nabataea into the Roman empire. The operation was carried out by A. Cornelius Palma from 105 to 106. Bostra became the capital of the new province called *Arabia*, and there followed a new era, starting on March 22, 106. The new capital became the seat of a Roman legion, the III Cyrenaica.

THE NABATAEANS: THEIR NATIONAL GOD

The inscriptions permit a fair analysis of the Nabataean religion.[45] Unlike most of the other nations in the Near East, the Nabataeans succeeded in maintaining their Arabic traditions and enjoyed an unusual independence; therefore their pantheon constitutes a standard reference for evaluating the religious life of other contemporary communities in the Syrian Desert.

[44] Arrian *Anabasis* 7. 20. 1. Strabo (16. 1. 11) noted that the two gods of the Arabs were Zeus and Dionysus. The latter was believed to have been the founder of *Dionysias* (the ancient Soada, site of the modern Suweida); see R. Dussaud, *Topographie historique de la Syrie antique et médiévale*, Bibliothèque archéologique et historique, IV (Paris: Paul Geuthner, 1927), p. 369. The identification of Dionysus with Dushara was reported by Isidorus of Charax (around A.D. 25) according to the testimony of Hesychius, a lexicographer of the fifth century A.D.; see A. D. Cook, *Zeus: A Study of Ancient Religion*, III (Cambridge: At the University Press, 1940), p. 912, note 1, and Sourdel, *Les cultes du Hauran*, p. 63.

[45] Starcky deals with the Nabataean religion in *Suppl. DB*, VII, cols. 985–1016. This remains the best comprehensive study of the subject.

A study of Nabataean personal names shows that the divine name *Ilah* was the one most frequently used to form theophores, but this, of course, is far from being characteristic. *Ilah* means "god," and it is cognate with proto-Semitic *il(u)* and with Northwest Semitic *el.* Whether *el* was originally a proper name or simply an appellative is not yet clear. Yet the question is of some importance to the history of religion in antiquity. In fact, should *el* be a proper name, its presence in proto-Semitic would emphasize the monotheistic character of the primitive religion of all Semites.[46]

The supreme god of the Nabataeans was Dushara; in Nabataean, Dushara means "the one" (*du*) of Shara (*šr'* being very likely either a toponym or the name of a tribe). Dushara was equated with Zeus. His role of supreme deity in the Nabataean pantheon receives its official acknowledgment in the inscriptions accompanying the offerings made by Syllaios, the prime minister of Obodas II, in the sanctuaries of Miletus and Delos. Syllaios (whose real title was "the brother of the king") visited these sanctuaries on his way to Rome, where eventually he was put to death by Augustus.

The identification of Dushara with Zeus does not, however, permit the conclusion that the Nabataeans thought of Dushara as a sort of Baal Shamin, for in a list of Nabataean gods Baal Shamin and Dushara are mentioned as different

[46] An important feature of the entire pre-Islamic onomastics is the overwhelming popularity of the element *'l* and *'lh* in Arabic proper names; see G. Lankester Harding's conclusions in his massive book (around 1,000 pages) *An Index and Concordance of Pre-Islamic Arabian Names and Inscriptions* (Toronto: University of Toronto Press, 1971). The root *'wl* is common Semitic, and it can be translated by "to be in front," "to lead," "first," "beginning," etc.; see D. Cohen, *Dictionnaire des racines sémitiques ou attestées dans les langues sémitiques*, fasc. 1 (Paris: Mouton, 1970), p. 12. *El* may have been used to indicate the tribe, the chief of the tribe, or even the god of the tribe; see J. Starcky, *Revue biblique* 67 (1960), 271. For the Mesopotamian texts, see J.J.M. Roberts, *The Earliest Semitic Pantheon: A Study of the Semitic Deities Attested in Mesopotamia Before Ur III* (Baltimore: Johns Hopkins University Press, 1972), pp. 32 ff.

deities.[47] That Beal Shamin and Dushara had not been identified by the Nabataeans implies that Baal Shamin was always considered by them as a foreign god. This is understandable. Baal Shamin was a god who took care of the crops, and his cult became popular whenever agriculture had begun to develop, as is well attested at Palmyra, at Dura-Europos, and in the Hauran. To be sure, the Nabataeans did not remain for centuries the nomadic tribes described by Diodorus of Sicily, and they changed their nomadic standards as Strabo, fifty years after Diodorus, clearly explains in his *Geography* (16. 4. 26). But the Nabataeans, amidst their opulence, remained attached to their primitive traditions, and their institutions, for all we know, were basically tribal. The agricultural activity of the Nabataeans must have been precarious, especially in the center of the kingdom, the region of Petra. This would explain why the cult of Baal Shamin never took root among them. The devotion to the god shown by some Nabataean tribes in the Hauran is to be explained as the result of their acceptance of a sedentary life.

The cult of Baal Shamin was not widespread in southern Nabataea; the most conspicuous of his epithets, however, appears in a funerary inscription of al-Ḥijr (Madāin Ṣāliḥ) that calls forth the Lord of the World against the would-be robber.[48] The expression *mr' 'lm'*, "Lord of the World," styles Baal Shamin at Palmyra and, at Qumran, is applied to God in the *Genesis Apocryphon*.[49] It can be understood as "Lord of the World" or "Lord of Eternity." The real meaning of this title eludes us. Nonetheless, the Semitic *mare 'alma* in the bilingual inscription from eṭ-Ṭayyibe proclaims the cosmic supremacy of Baal Shamin, thus overcoming the Greek title *megystos keraunios*, which reflects a

[47] Starcky, *Suppl. DB*, VII, col. 993.

[48] A. J. Jaussen and R. Savignac, *Mission archéologique en Arabie*, I (Paris: E. Leroux, 1909), pp. 172–176.

[49] J. A. Fitzmyer, *The Genesis Apocryphon of Qumran Cave I: A Commentary* (Rome: Pontifical Biblical Institute, 1966), p. 75.

more restrained conception of the deity.[50] In the Nabataean inscription of al-Ḥijr *mare 'alma* is used not as an epithet but as a proper name. This stresses the monotheistic connotation of this theological term. The fact is of particular interest because another inscription from the same region seems, again, to point out a monotheistic trend in the beliefs of the North Arabian Nabataeans. The inscription carved at the entrance of a tomb, states who the owners of the two niches are and ends by calling upon "the one who separates night from day" to curse those who would take away the corpses.[51] The expression "the one who separates night from day" stands by itself, but most probably it is to be referred to Dushara, whose name is invoked in many other funerary inscriptions from the same area. Only a supreme god is entitled to claim the right of separating night from day. Indeed, it is the epithet of a creator god like the biblical Yahweh, whose first act as creator was to separate light from darkness. With this descriptive expression Dushara's preeminence in the Nabataean pantheon seems to be fully acknowledged.

THE CULT OF ALTARS AMONG THE NABATAEANS

Dushara was also adored under the appellation of Dushara-A'ra. This title reveals a great deal about Arab religiosity. A'ra was the name of the idol of Bostra from the very beginning of Nabataean history. When Rabbel II made Bostra his royal residence a few years before the creation of the province of Arabia, the Nabataean ruler must have assimilated the cult of Dushara, the national god, to that of the local idol of Bostra. A'ra was represented by what can be called in Nabataean a *mesgida*. This term means both "altar" and "holy place," but among the Nabataeans it seems to have been used as meaning either "altar" or "idol." A'ra (' 'r') is transcribed in Greek *Aarras*. We are

50 See above, pp. 28–29.
51 Jaussen and Savignac, I, pp. 142–145.

informed about this Greek pronunciation by a bilingual inscription from Umm el-Jimal. On the other hand, the usual change of Arabic *ghain* into Aramaic *'ain* makes likely the hypothesis that A'ra comes from an Arabic root *gh-r-y*, "to dye"; *gharrā*, "object dyed." Etymologically the name A'ra would mean an altar or idol dyed with the blood of the victims offered upon it. Moreover, the entry of the lexicographer of Suidas on the word *Theusares* is relevant. He says that the name means "the god" (*theos*) Ares (of Petra), an idol of black stone, quadrangular in form, upon which the Arabs sprinkled the blood of sacrificed animals.[52] A curious passage in Porphyry's *De abstinentia* (2. 56) informs us that certain tribes of Arabia slaughtered children upon the altar, which in turn was worshiped as an idol.

The cult of the god "altar" is well attested in North Syria, where, according to Greek inscriptions, he is known as the god *Madbachos* or the god *Bomos* (the latter is the Greek word for the Semitic *madbaḥ*).[53] Related to the cult of the "altar" is that of *mesgida* at Elephantine, where the *mesgida* seems to indicate "the place of cult" rather than "the altar." Among the Jews of Elephantine oaths were taken by the god *mesgida*;[54] this cult is similar to that of *ḥerem-bethel*, "Sanctuary of Bethel," or to those of "Temple of Nabu," "Temple of Bethel," etc., attested in the fifth-century Aramaic papyri from Hermoupolis.[55] During the second and third centuries of our era a god "sanctuary" was adored under the name *Tur-mesgida*, wherein the element *ṭur*, "mountain," points to the cult of a mountain god.[56]

[52] Starcky, *Suppl. DB*, VII, cols. 988–989.

[53] J. T. Milik, "Les papyrus araméens d'Hermoupolis et les cultes syrophéniciens en Égypte perse," *Biblica* 48 (1967), 578, where the texts are quoted and commented upon.

[54] See B. Porten, *Archives from Elephantine* (Berkeley and Los Angeles: University of California Press, 1968), pp. 155–156, for a discussion of the term.

[55] Milik, *Biblica* 48 (1967), 565 ff.   [56] Ibid., pp. 579–580.

The cult of the altars formed part of the religious practices of the Semites. The Arabs of Syria and North Arabia could hardly be an exception, and the excavations of Palmyra and Hatra conclusively prove that the inhabitants of the two cities were strongly predisposed to dedicate altars. Hundreds of them have been uncovered there. At Hatra they are called *mkn'*. This term comes from *kwn*, "to stand," or "to be firm in a place," and conveys the impression that the altar was offered as an ex-voto in a fixed place from which it could not be removed.[57] At Paymyra, most of the altars were dedicated to the god "whose name is blessed for ever," and they, too, had the character of ex-votos. Each altar represented an offering by itself, regardless of whether incense was burned on it or not.[58]

A theological attitude similar to the one which made the altar an object of worship developed with respect to the baetyls.[59] The Nabataean baetyls of Petra, al-Ḥijr, and the Hauran are in general rectangular stones, sometimes standing on a throne, or *motab*. Both the baetyl and the motab were worshiped. This, however, is not a particular feature of the Nabataean religion. We have already seen that the gods Bethel and Anat-Bethel were invoked in Assyrian times (see pp. 30f). The popularity of the baetyl as the residence of the god—or, rather, of the stone as the place in which the god was embodied—remained alive in the Near East until Christian times, for in the third century of our era an altar at Dura-Europos was still dedicated to Zeus Betylos.[60]

OTHER CULTS AMONG THE NABATAEANS

The cult of a supreme god seems to have existed among the Nabataeans since the beginning of their nomadic life.

[57] J. Teixidor, "The Altars Found at Hatra," *Sumer* 21 (1965), 85–92.

[58] See below, pp. 122 ff.

[59] Starcky, *Suppl. DB*, VII, cols. 1008–1013.

[60] H. Seyrig in M. I. Rostovtzeff, ed., *The Excavations at Dura-Europos*, IV (New Haven: Yale University Press, 1933), pp. 68–71, no. 168.

It is possible that Dushara, "the one of Shara," is but the epithet of Ruḍa, the ancestral god of the North Arabian tribes. Indeed, the epigraphical evidence supports an identification of Ruḍa with the planet Mercury. To the Bedouin, the cult of Mercury meant the worship of the familiar star which divided night from day, a function that befitted Dushara in his quality of ruler of the world.[61] But for a Nabataean installed in the Hauran Dushara was better identified with Dionysus, whose cult remained understandably absent from the North Arabian inscriptions (see p. 70 and n. 18). The gifts of Dionysus obviously are lacking in the desert, where the cult of the stars becomes paramount. Other Nabataean tribes appear to have worshiped a god called *Shai‘ al qaum*, i.e., "the one who leads the people." This cult is attested in the Safaitic inscriptions.[62] The divine name appears on the wall opposite the Diwan of al-Ḥijr in North Arabia.[63] A Nabataean inscription from the Hauran dated in the twenty-sixth year of king Rabbel II, i.e., A.D. 96, commemorates the offering made by an Arab to this god.[64] A Palmyrene inscription records the dedication of two altars to Shai‘ al qaum. The offering is made by a Nabataean horseman, ‘Ubaidu son of ‘Animu son of Sa‘adallat. The dedication precisely says: "To Shai‘ al qaum,

[61] Starcky, *Suppl. DB*, VII, cols. 990–996; see also his article "Relief dédié au dieu Mun‘im," *Semitica* 22 (1972), 57–65, where he rightly identifies Ruḍa (i.e., Orotalt or Arṣu) with Mercury. In his Oration 4 (see note 13) Julian says that the people of Edessa worshiped the Sun flanked by Azizos and Monimos (Hermes). Thus Monimos is the planet Mercury that precedes the sunrise. Monimos, from Arabic *mun‘im*, "the favorable one," is another name for Ruḍa. The astral character of the Edessean religion may mirror a late theological reflection on the ancient Arab cults of the desert by which the planets Mercury and Venus were believed to be identical with the ancestral pair of male and female deities.

[62] He is frequently mentioned as *s‘hqm*.

[63] Jaussen and Savignac, I, p. 221; for the Diwan, "le grand sanctuaire de Hégrâ," see pp. 405–421.

[64] R. Dussaud and F. Macler, *Voyage archéologique au Ṣafâ et dans le Djebel ed-Druz* (Paris: E. Leroux, 1901), pp. 187–188.

the good and bountiful god, who does not drink wine."[65] The inscription is dated in September, 132 of our era. The dedicatory formula clearly defines Shai' al qaum as a god of nomads among whom the drinking of wine was not customary, if not forbidden altogether, as Diodorus of Sicily (19. 94. 3) says it was among the Nabataean nomads. The only known representation of the god was found in a Palmyrene tessera, where Shai' al qaum wears a helmet.[66] This martial aspect of the god suits his character as "leader" of the people. He appears as the protector of the caravans, and in this respect a parallel can be drawn between him and the angel of Yahweh in Exodus 23:20, 23. Shai' al qaum, thus, would not have been a god of the Zeus type—like Baal Shamin, Hadad, or Dushara—but, rather, his angel. The idea, nonetheless, reverts to the belief in a supreme deity.

Theophorous names found in inscriptions from North Arabia, southern Palestine, Egypt, and the Hauran reveal the existence of the cult of Qos. This epigraphical material can be dated to the third and second centuries B.C. Qos certainly was known in Assyrian times, for the Edomite king during Tiglathpileser III's reign was called Kausmalak ("Qos is king"). Later on, under Esarhaddon, another king of Edom bore the name Kausgabri ("Qos is mighty").[67] The Nabataeans venerated Qos in the sanctuary of Khirbet Tannur, in Transjordan. A Nabataean inscription on a broken limestone stele reads: "(The stele) which Qosmalak made for Qos, the god of *ḥwrw*." Here, *ḥwrw* is probably a toponym formed from the root *ḥrw*, "to burn." Opposite to Khirbet Tannur, on the northern side of the Wadi Hesa, there is a dark basalt outcrop of volcanic origin. Qos must

---

[65] Cooke, *North-Semitic Inscriptions* (cited in note 24 above), p. 304; *CISem.*, II, 3978.

[66] H. Ingholt, H. Seyrig, J. Starcky, and A. Caquot, *Recueil des tessères de Palmyre*, Bibliothèque archéologique et historique, LVIII (Paris: Paul Geuthner, 1955), p. 46, no. 332.

[67] The various references are collected in Teixidor, BES 1972, no. 47.

have been known as the god of this denudate region, for another Nabataean inscription simply calls him *ḥwrwy*, which can be translated as "the one of *ḥwrw*."[68]

Qos, at Khirbet Tannur, is represented seated on a throne flanked by bulls and holding in his left hand a multi-branched thunderbolt, the symbol of the lord of rain. At Bostra, an inscription in Greek and Nabataean commemorates the offering of an eagle to him.[69] The bulls, the thunderbolt, and the eagle seem to support the conclusion that Qos was a weather god.

Josephus, in his *Jewish Antiquities* (15. 253), says that the ancestor of Kosgobarus ("Qos is mighty"), the governor of Idumaea and Gaza during the reign of Herod, had been a priest of *Koze*. Josephus certainly is not giving a wrong spelling of the name of Qos but, rather, reporting the divine name as it was known in Idumaea. Here the national god, under Nabataean influence, must have become identified with Quzah, "the archer," a deity of the North Arabian pantheon who was worshiped as a mountain and a weather god. The term *qšt* (root *qwš*?) means "bow," and this might have helped to identify Qos with the Arab god of the rainbow (*qaws quzaḥ*).

In Idumaea the cult of Apollo seems to have been associated with that of Qos. Both divine names are overwhelmingly attested in the personal names of the Idumaeans who lived at Memphis and at Hermoupolis during the second and the first centuries B.C.[70] A stele from Memphis, from the middle of the second century B.C., commemorates the dedication by the Idumaeans of a temple to Apollo and Zeus. Even though we do not know for which Semitic deity Zeus stands in the text, it is very likely that he was

[68] J. T. Milik, *Syria* 35 (1958), 237–238, has published the two inscriptions. For the archaeological remains of Khirbet Tannur, see N. Glueck, *Deities and Dolphins* (New York: Farrar, Straus and Giroux, 1965). Starcky has written an important review of this book in *Revue biblique* 75 (1968), 206–235; see especially p. 209.

[69] Milik, *Syria* 35 (1958), 236.   [70] Teixidor, BES 1972, no. 47.

Qos. A similar instance occurs at Marissa, the capital of Idumaea, a territory to the south of Judaea which was occupied by those Edomite tribes who had been pushed out of their homeland by the invading Nabataeans. The archaeological excavations carried out at Marissa uncovered several tombs decorated in accordance with Hellenistic taste. The names of the owners of the tombs reveal the presence of a strong Sidonian colony.[71] This fact is by no means surprising. The Sidonians had been in the neighboring regions since the fifth century B.C.[72] In the closing centuries of the first millennium B.C. they had stretched their area of influence to the interior of the country and assimilated themselves into the local culture. Many names recovered from the tombs are in fact theophorous of Qos. In turn, these Sidonians must have propagated the cult of Apollo, a Greek deity whose counterpart was the Phoenician god Reshef.[73]

The Nabataeans, like other Semitic peoples, named their gods after the places where they were worshiped. The best-known example, of course, is that of Dushara, the national god, but other examples are equally interesting and show that the deities were inseparable from their sanctuaries. A Greek inscription from Sammet el-Baradan, in the Hauran,

[71] See J. P. Peters and H. Thiersch, *Painted Tombs in the Necropolis of Marissa* (London: Palestine Exploration Fund, 1905), pp. 38–71, and F. M. Abel, *Revue biblique* 34 (1925), 267–275.

[72] According to a Phoenician inscription from Sidon, the Persian king gave the territories of Dor, Jaffa, and the plain of Sharon to Eshmun'azar, king of Sidon; see *KAI* 14. For recent studies on the date of this inscription, see Teixidor, BES 1969, no. 83.

[73] The identification of Reshef with Apollo is explicitly attested in many Phoenician inscriptions from Cyprus. As far as southern Palestine is concerned such an identification must have been familiar to its inhabitants, for the Arab village of *Arsuf*, near Jaffa, was known in Seleucid times as *Apollonia*.

mentions the god *Ilaalgê*, which is a mere transcription of *'Ilâh al-Gê*, i.e., "the god of al-Ge." The toponym corresponds to the modern el-Ǧî, the site of the first Nabataean capital at the entrance of el-Siq, in the Wadi Musa.[74] The god is explicitly identified with Dushara,[75] and the popularity of his name is shown in such personal names as *Amatelge* ("Servant of el-Ge") and *Abdalge*, where the toponym itself, *el-Ge,* became a divine name.

Another conspicuous example of this transference of meaning in a toponym appears in a bilingual inscription from Si'a. The Greek text says: "Seeia standing in the Hauranite land"; the Nabataean inscription runs as follows: "This is the image (*ṣlmt'*) of *š'y'w*."[76] The form *ṣlmt'* indicates that the statue was that of a female deity, presumably Tyche. The term *š'y'*, which probably means "leveled square," was given to the goddess, who personified the holiness of the area where the great sanctuary of Baal Shamin had been constructed.[77]

As a people the Nabataeans were of composite stock and eventually occupied different cultural environments, one agricultural and sedentary, the other nomadic and accessible to the caravan trade. These diversities explain the somewhat contradictory descriptions of this folk that Diodorus of Sicily and Strabo handed down to us.

Diodorus, for instance, knew that the Nabataeans ranged "over a country which is partly desert and partly waterless,

74 Milik, *Dédicaces*, pp. 428–429.

75 A. Negev, *Israel Exploration Journal* 13 (1963), 113–124; J. Starcky, in *Revue biblique* 64 (1957), 205, and in his article in *Suppl. DB*, VII, col. 987.

76 Littmann, *Semitic Inscriptions*, sect. A: *Nabataean Inscriptions*, pp. 81–83, no. 103.

77 Littmann, ibid., p. 82, indicates some theophorus names of the goddess. The deification of a holy enceinte is found at Elephantine; see above, p. 86.

though a small section of it is fruitful." In his time they led "a life of brigandage" and used to pillage "a large part of the neighbouring territory."[78] Around the Gulf of 'Aqaba, the Nabataeans occupied "a large part of the coast and not a little of the country which stretches inland." They had flocks and herds "in multitudes beyond belief."[79] They lived in the open air, "claiming as native land a wilderness that has neither rivers nor abundant springs from which it is possible for a hostile army to obtain water." Diodorus explicitly says that "it is their custom neither to plant grain, set out any fruit-bearing trees, use wine, nor construct any house; and if any one is found acting contrary to this, death is his penalty." The Nabataeans, though, are wealthy, "for not a few of them are accustomed to bring down to the sea frankincense and myrrh and the most valuable kinds of spices, which they procure from those who convey them from what is called Arabia Eudaemon." But some Nabataean tribes were not involved in the caravan trade nor did they practice nomadic life; on the contrary, "they tilled the soil," mingled "with the tribute-paying peoples," and had the same customs "as the Syrians."[80] Diodorus must have had in mind those tribes that inhabited the Hauran.

In contrast with this description, Strabo gives the following information about Petra: "Petra is always ruled by some king from the royal family; and the king has as administrator one of his companions, who is called brother. It is exceedingly well governed." On the authority of his friend Athenodorus, Strabo says that "many Romans and many other foreigners" sojourned at Petra and often engaged themselves "in lawsuits" both with one another and with the natives, "but that none of the natives prosecuted one another, and that they in every way kept peace with

[78] Diod. 2. 48. 1–2; trans. Oldfather, Loeb, pp. 41–43.

[79] Diod. 3. 43. 4; trans. Oldfather, Loeb, pp. 213–215.

[80] Diod. 19. 94. 2–5; trans. R. M. Geer, Loeb Classical Library (Cambridge, Mass., 1966), pp. 87–89.

one another."[81] All this shows how important traditions were among the Nabataeans; furthermore, it indicates that rights were warranted by usage, which emphasizes the tribal character of Nabataean institutions. It is equally interesting to note that the king always came from the same dynastic family, which indicates that a hierarchy of familes existed in the town. On the other hand, the Nabataeans had accepted the way of living of the settled people, for Strabo notes that "they are so much inclined to acquire possessions that they publicly fine anyone who has diminished his possessions and also confer honors on anyone who has increased them." This I would consider as indicative of the Nabataean drive to strengthen their settlement in the region of Petra. Caravan traders, nomads, and newly settled tillers, all made it possible for that country to be "well supplied with fruits,"[82] a fact that seems to have surprised Strabo.

The picture of the Nabataeans drawn by the Classical writers is that of a people with a strong nomadic background but aiming at the establishment of a well-administered kingdom. This endeavor, however, was never fulfilled because Nabataea was made a Roman province in 106, and eventually other Arab tribes took over the Nabataean lands, especially in North Arabia. Perhaps the lack of cultural unity explains the existence of a great variety of cults among the Nabataeans.

Arab Cults in Southern Palestine: Gaza and Ascalon

At the beginning of the Ptolemaic period the coastal region of southern Palestine was to a great extent in the hands of Arab tribes, who became responsible for the local markets as well as for the Arabian trade routes leading to southern Palestine and spreading from there over Syria and

[81] Strabo *Geography* 16. 4. 21; trans. H. L. Jones, Loeb Classical Library (Cambridge, Mass., 1966), p. 353.

[82] Strabo 16. 4. 26; trans. Jones, Loeb, pp. 367–369.

Egypt. The Zenon papyri are an invaluable source of information regarding this caravan traffic. These documents from the third century B.C. constituted part of the archives of Zenon, the agent of the Apollonius who was finance minister for Egypt.[83] Communications took place by sea, but land routes also were in use. Products from Syria reached Egypt via Gaza and Ascalon, two cities that became connecting links not only for North Arabia, Syria, and Egypt but also for the land of Punt on the Somali coast and the South Arabian territories. Incense, of course, was the first and most important product traded, but slaves, grain, wine, cheese, salted fish-meat, honey, etc., constituted important commodities. The area seems to have enjoyed a certain political freedom owing to its geographical position. The Seleucids never recognized the right of the Ptolemies to govern Palestine, and this means that the Egyptian monarchs took especial care to gain the sympathies of its people by trying "to meet, as far as possible, the economic-political demands of the natives" in order to keep them under Egyptian rule.[84]

In Gaza or Ascalon agriculture was not an indispensable way of life. These maritime cities had a population of Arab Bedouin dedicated to international trade and on the basis of Herodotus (3. 5) would now be considered buffer zones between Palestine, Phoenicia, and Egypt. In 332 B.C., when Alexander the Great arrived at Gaza, Betis was the kinglet in command of the fortress under the supervision of the Persians. Hegesias called Betis *Basileus*,[85] and indeed he must have had good control of the population because he was capable of organizing a force of ten thousand men against Alexander. Arrian says that the Arab mercenaries formed part of the army; this information is corroborated

---

[83] V. Tscherikover, "Palestine under the Ptolemies: A Contribution to the Study of the Zenon Papyri," in *Mizraim* 4–5 (1937), 9–90.

[84] Ibid., pp. 27, 40, 56.

[85] F. M. Abel, "Les confins de la Palestine et de l'Égypte sous les Ptolémées," *Revue biblique* 48 (1939), 531.

by Quintus Curtius.[86] Later on, when Diodorus describes the arrival of Antigonus in the city on his way to Egypt,[87] we hear about the presence of Arab Bedouin in the region of Gaza. Gaza furnished Antigonus's army with food for ten days, and the Arabs procured him a great number of camels to transport it. This information, by the way, underlines the city's character as an important commercial center.

We know little about the religious life of the area. The existence of a cult of *Palaistine Aphrodite Urania* is attested in the dedication made by an Ascalonite living at Delos, and so is the cult of Poseidon. Aphrodite was called *Derceto*, a term which probably means "mighty." Both Diodorus and Strabo mention her name.[88] Herodotus reports that the temple of this Aphrodite was "the most ancient of all the temples of this goddess." And he adds: "The one in Cyprus the Cyprians themselves admit was derived from it" (1. 105).[89] To this scanty information, the coins of Ascalon from the time of Augustus and throughout the imperial series add representations of a deity called *Phanebal*.[90] The god appears wearing a helmet and a cuirass and holding in his right hand a *harpe* (spear); in his left hand he supports a circular shield and a long palm branch. In the latest coins Phanebal is shown with his right hand raised.[91] A youthful and warlike god, his name is to be interpreted as "the Face of Baal," a title which the goddess

[86] Arrian *Anab.* 2. 25. 4. For Q. Curtius, see his *History of Alexander* 4. 6.

[87] Diod. 20. 73. 3.

[88] Diod. 2. 4. 1–3; Strabo 16. 4. 27. For the term, see Teixidor, BES 1972, no. 62.

[89] Herodotus, *The Histories*, trans. Aubrey de Sélincourt (Baltimore: Penguin Books, 1968), pp. 56–57.

[90] In *Yahweh and the Gods of Canaan* (New York: Doubleday, 1968), pp. 129 and 242, note 101, W. F. Albright thought that the name designated an "androgynous" deity. See also H. Seyrig's article "Les dieux armés et les Arabes en Syrie," in *Syria* 47 (1970), 96–97, where the representation of the god is discussed.

[91] G. F. Hill, *A Catalogue of the Greek Coins in the British Museum: Palestine* (hereafter *BMC: Palestine*) (London, 1914), pp. lix–lxi.

Tenit bears in the Phoenician sites along the North African coast. At Ascalon it was obviously applied to a male divinity. The term *pane-* merely indicates the function of the god as a messenger of Baal. It is altogether possible that the people of Ascalon had identified Phanebal with Apollo, since the cult of the latter was well accepted in the city.[92]

The religious life of the inhabitants of Gaza is better known. The coins here seem to confirm literary sources. Among the imperial coins of the city there is one, of the time of Hadrian, that shows the figure of a nude Apolline god standing beside a goddess, probably Artemis. The two deities are within a temple, which is indicated on the coin by two columns supporting an architrave and a pediment.[93] On the other hand, the author of the biography of Gaza's bishop Porphyry has left interesting information about the pagan cults of the people. This document, which was written by Marcus the Deacon, probably during the fifth century, mentions the cult of Marnas and his famous temple. It is likely that the temple represented on the coins was the *Marneion*. The origin of the name *Marnas* is unknown; the only information regarding this deity comes from Marcus, who says that the god was "a Cretan-born Zeus."[94] This may explain the youthful character of the god. His name is given by the legend on the coins: *Gaza Marna*. Sometimes a Phoenician *mem* is used as an adjunct in the field or as a main type. The *mem* must stand for the name of the god. In the narrative of Marcus the god is presented as a Zeus called upon by the pagans of Gaza to relieve their city from a dramatic drought in much the same way that the god of Mount Carmel had been invoked centuries earlier.[95] The colossal statue of a Zeus found near Gaza at the end of the

[92] Julius Africanus says that Herod descended from a hierodule of the temple of Apollo at Ascalon; see Eusebius *Ecclesiastical History* 1. 6. 2 and 1. 7. 11.

[93] Hill, *BMC: Palestine*, pp. lxxv–lxxvi.

[94] See the translation by G. F. Hill, *The Life of Porphyry, Bishop of Gaza, by Marcus the Deacon* (Oxford: Clarendon Press, 1913).

[95] Ibid., chs. 19 and 20.

nineteenth century may well have been a portrayal of Marnas.[96] This may be the supreme god represented on the coins by a head of Zeus.

The cult of Marnas most probably succeeded that of Dagon, the god of the Philistines. According to Judges 16:23 and 1 Samuel 5:2-5 Dagon was worshiped at Gaza and Ashdod; the royal inscription of Eshmun'azar of Sidon mentioned him as the god of the plain of Sharon (*KAI* 14); moreover, some Palestinian place-names contain the element *dgn* which indicates that they were centers of his cult.[97] Dagon is the Palestinian version of the Amorite Dagan whose cult spread from Mesopotamia to the Mediterranean coast. Dagan became prominent in the pantheon of Ugarit to the extent that some scholars maintain that he had been identified with El.[98] Nothing definite, however, is known of Dagon in the Philistine lands. The character of fertility god often attributed to him is based on the meaning of the word *dagan*, "grain," in Hebrew and Phoenician. Philo himself used this facile etymology, which is not supported by Ugaritic texts. The cult of Dagon persisted until the middle of the second century B.C., for 1 Maccabees 10:83-84 reports that Jonathan, after defeating the army of Apollonius at Ashdod burned the city and the temple of Dagon in which some natives had taken shelter.

The epigraphical materials so far studied offer a disparate picture of the cults favored by the Arab tribes by the end of the first millennium B.C. and the first centuries of the

[96] Hill, *BMC: Palestine*, p. lxxi, note 2.

[97] F. M. Abel, *Géographie de la Palestine*, Vol. II, 3rd ed. (Paris: J. Gabalda, 1967), p. 269.

[98] A. Caquot, M. Sznycer and A. Herdner, *Textes Ougaritiques. Tome I: Mythes et légendes*, Littératures anciennes du Proche-Orient, 7 (Paris: Les éditions du Cerf, 1974), pp. 52-54; the authors reject the identification proposed by A. Kapelrud, U. Cassuto, and J. Fontenrose; see p. 53, note 1.

Christian era. The lack of a common religious life is not surprising because the land they inhabited, the Syrian Desert, the Hauran, the coastal towns of southern Palestine, and North Arabia, did not form a geographical or political unity.

Palmyra constitutes an outstanding exception to this situation: the city was the capital of a geographically well-defined territory. The commercial activity of Palmyra, lying on one of the main routes of the caravan trade, offered a propitious atmosphere for syncretistic forms of cult. At the same time, her social structures, shaped in a somewhat oligarchic fashion, imposed patterns on the entire religious life of the city and the neighboring territories. The homogeneous character of the religious inscriptions found there will be analyzed in the following chapter.

FOUR

THE SUPREME GOD OF PALMYRA

PALMYRA is in the center of an oasis on the northwest edge of the Arabian Desert. The site is culturally and economically linked to the main Syrian areas: the plain of the Hauran, Damascus, Homs (ancient Emesa), Hama, and Aleppo. Since ancient times Palmyra has maintained close relations with settlements lying on the Euphrates River between the modern towns of Deir ez-Zôr and Hit. Ancient Palmyra lived by trade; consequently, her market was open to all kinds of commodities from Babylon, the Persian Gulf, and Arabia. The ancient Tariff of Palmyra established the taxes to be levied on the import and export of slaves, purple-dyed fleeces, dried fruits, perfumes, oil, fat, salted fish, skins, wool, pine cones, herbs, salt, prostitutes, and bronze statues. Palmyra, as a caravan city, counted in the economic life of the ancient Near East during the entire first millennium B.C., and when the Romans established themselves on the Syrian coast in the first century B.C., the role of Palmyra as a commercial crossroad increased in importance in the agitated world of that day.

Palmyra is the Greco-Roman name of the city. The modern Arabic name *Tudmor* derives from the very old form *Tadmor* (also *Tadmer, Tadmar, Tadmur*) found in the cuneiform texts. The first mention of Tadmor goes back to an Assyrian tablet from Cappadocia, to be dated in the nineteenth century B.C.[1] A hundred years later the Tad-

---

[1] See G. Eisser and J. Lewy, *Die altassyrischen Rechtsurkunden vom Kültepe*, 3–4, *Mitteilungen der Vorderasiatisch-Ägyptischen Gesellschaft* 35, pt. 3 (Leipzig, 1935), pp. 18–21, no. 303. Assyrian contacts with Asia Minor since the twentieth century B.C. are well attested by the clay tablets found at Kültepe. The documents, written in cuneiform, deal

moreans are mentioned in two letters from Mari.[2] These documents suggest that the inhabitants of Tadmor were Amorites. The Amorites were the western Semites mentioned by Sumerians and Akkadians since the twenty-first century B.C. Their presence at Palmyra is not surprising, for Amorite tribes occupied the North Syrian cities during the entire second millennium B.C. About 1100 B.C. the Assyrian king Tiglathpileser I organized a military expedition against the Syrian hinterland. The Assyrian *Chronicle*, in the usual first person, describes the events in the following manner: "Twenty-eight times (I fought) the Ahlamu peoples and the Arameans, (once) I even crossed the Euphrates twice in one year. I defeated them from Tadmar (Palmyra) which (lies) in the country Amurru, Anat which (lies) in the country Suhu, as far as the town Rapiqu which (lies) in Kar-Duniash (i.e., Babylonia). I brought their possessions as spoils to my town Ashur."[3]

---

with economics. The merchandise transported by the Assyrian caravans from Ashur into Asia Minor consisted primarily of textiles and lead; see H. Lewy in the *Cambridge Ancient History*, 3rd ed., I, pt. 2 (Cambridge: At the University Press, 1971), pp. 724–726. Wool, copper, silver, and gold were the commodities traded by the Assyrians. For the Assyrian trade in general, see M. T. Larsen, *Old Assyrian Caravan Procedures* (Istanbul: Nederlands Historisch-Archaeologisch Instituut in het Nabije Oosten, 1967). Puzur-Ishtar of *Tadmor*, the person mentioned on the Assyrian tablet from Kültepe, was most probably an Amorite.

[2] See G. Dossin, *Correspondance de Iasmaḫ-Addu*, Archives royales de Mari, V (Paris: Imprimerie Nationale, 1952), p. 40, no. 23. One of these letters deals with the attacks of the Sutu nomads on Tadmor; see J.-R. Kupper, *Les nomades en Mésopotamie au temps des rois de Mari*, Bibliothèque de la Faculté de Philosophie et Lettres de l'Université de Liège, CXLII (Paris: Société d'Éditions "Les Belles Lettres," 1966), pp. 84 and 93. For the second letter, see G. Dossin, "Quelques textes inédits de Mari," *Comptes rendus de la première rencontre assyriologique internationale (Paris, 26–28 juin 1950)* (Leiden: E. J. Brill, 1951), pp. 19–21; J. Starcky, "Palmyre," in *Suppl. DB*, VI (Paris: Letouzey & Ané, 1960), col. 1078.

[3] *ANET*, p. 275.

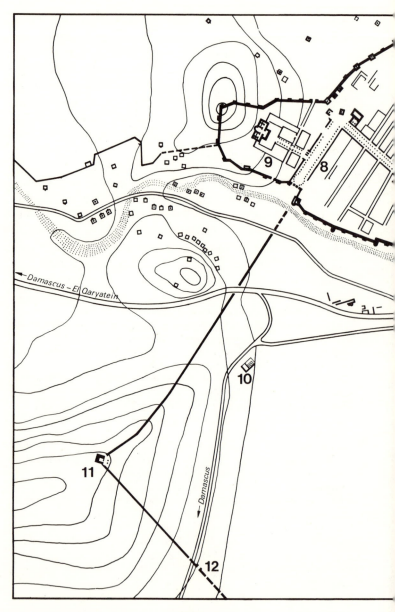

MAP III

Plan of Palmyra

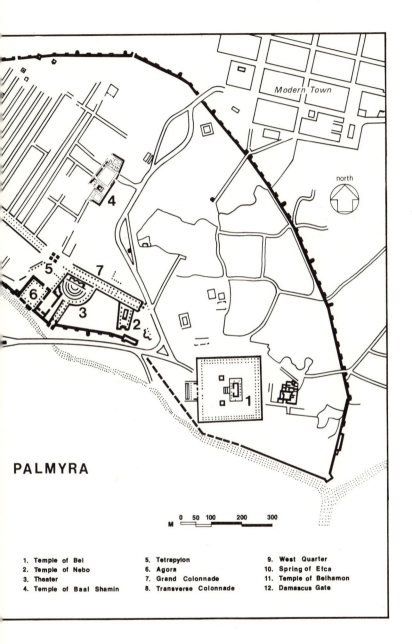

PALMYRA

0 50 100   200   300
M

1. Temple of Bel
2. Temple of Nebo
3. Theater
4. Temple of Baal Shamin
5. Tetrapylon
6. Agora
7. Grand Colonnade
8. Transverse Colonnade
9. West Quarter
10. Spring of Efca
11. Temple of Belhamon
12. Damascus Gate

Modern Town

north

By the time of Tiglathpileser's campaigns only the name of the Amorites remained at Palmyra, for the Aramaeans were putting pressure on the fringes of the civilized world. The Aramaeans were a seminomadic group of Semitic extraction, who finally established an empire of their own by the ninth century B.C. Their presence at Palmyra is well documented both in the pantheon of the city and in the personal names of the citizens. Archaeological remains, however, are practically nonexistent there for the first part of the first millennium B.C.[4]

Tadmor probably developed as an important trade center under the Achaemenids, and during the Seleucid period the city was already prosperous. The Greek rulers in the Near East inherited the administrative system of the provinces from the Persians; it is thus understandable that Palmyra could increase her commercial activity. Appian describes the Palmyrenes as "merchants" who "bring the products of India and Arabia from Persia and dispose of them in the Roman territory."[5] A name recorded by the Greek historian Polybius[6] furnishes an interesting sidelight on pre-Roman Palmyra. A participant in the battle of Raphia (217 B.C.), in which Antiochus III was defeated by the

---

[4] Some of the objects deposited in a tomb found in the temple of Baal Shamin are to be dated in the second century B.C.; see R. Fellman, *Le sanctuaire de Baalshamin à Palmyre*, v: *Die Grabenlage*, Bibliotheca helvetica romana, x (Neuchâtel: P. Attinger, 1970), pp. 118–119, and C. Dunant, ibid., III: *Les inscriptions*, ibid., x (ibid., 1971), pp. 72–75. Before this date the archaeological information is practically nil. The conclusions regarding Palmyra during the third and the second millennia B.C. drawn by R. du Mesnil du Buisson from his archaeological survey, in which the present writer participated in November 1965, are very questionable; see du Mesnil du Buisson's report, "Première campagne de fouilles à Palmyre," *Académie des Inscriptions et Belles-Lettres, Comptes rendus des séances de l'année 1966*, 181–186, and M. Gawlikowski, *Le temple palmyrénien*, Palmyre, vi (Warsaw, 1973), pp. 18 and 53–54.

[5] Appian *The Civil Wars* 5. 9; trans. H. White, Loeb Classical Library (Cambridge, Mass., 1961), IV, p. 391.

[6] Polybius *The Histories* 5. 79. 8.

Egyptians, was an Arab sheikh who had recruited ten thousand soldiers to help the Greek monarch. This general was called *Zabdibel*, a name which means "gift of Bel." The element *zbd* appears in Aramaean and South Arabian names, and it certainly represents a very ancient term in Aramaic. The presence of the divine name Bel, designating a god whose cult was paramount in Palmyra, makes almost certain the conclusion that the sheikh was a Palmyrene Arab.[7]

The influx of Arab tribes into Palmyra should be understood as part of the wave of Nabataeans who invaded the Hauran and Damascus.[8] After the settlement of Amorites and Aramaeans, the arrival of Arabs in the area made Palmyra the center of major Semitic groups to whom Aramaic, by then an international language, must have served as a common link.

By 130 B.C. the Parthians had extended over the territory from the Euphrates to the Indus Valley. But in 64 B.C. Pompey made Syria a Roman province. Palmyra was not annexed. In 41 B.C. the city still maintained her independence, "being on the frontier between the Romans and the Parthians."[9] Palmyra seems to have been much influenced by Parthian culture. The archaeological excavations undertaken by the French Mission before World War II uncovered monuments which show pure Greco-Oriental ele-

---

[7] The name exists only at Palmyra; see J. Starcky, *Syria* 26 (1949), 39–40.

[8] For the presence of Nabataeans at Palmyra, see Milik, *Dédicaces*, pp. 211–212, and J. Teixidor, "The Nabataean Presence at Palmyra," in *The Gaster Festschrift: The Journal of the Ancient Near Eastern Society of Columbia University* 5 (New York, 1973), 405–409. One of the earliest personal names known from the inscriptions is *qynw*; see Dunant, *Les inscriptions*, p. 72, no. 60, line 4. The name is common among the Nabataeans; see Cantineau, *Le Nabatéen*, II (Paris: E. Leroux, 1932), p. 142. It is also common among other North Arabs; see I. Rabinowitz, "Aramaic inscriptions of the Fifth Century B.C.E. from a North-Arab Shrine in Egypt," *Journal of Near Eastern Studies* 15 (1956), 5–6.

[9] Appian as cited in note 5 above.

ments.[10] An inscription found in the temple of Bel mentions the existence of "the priests of Bel" as early as 44 B.C.[11] The temple itself was constructed according to Oriental patterns. Traditions in art at Palmyra reflect an influence coming from Seleucia-on-the-Tigris rather than from Antioch.[12] This favorable attitude toward the East is corroborated by the Palmyrene temple of Dura-Europos.[13] What happened in art parallels the process of transformation undergone by religious beliefs: under Babylonian influence the local god Bol had become Bel and formed a trinity with the two ancestral gods of Palmyra, following the Babylonian trend toward arranging deities in groups.

As to international trade under the Parthians, it should be remembered that the Parthians "emerged primarily as middlemen rather than as producers,"[14] and Palmyra was integrated into their trade policy. It is important to mention here the commercial contacts established by the Parthians with China before the end of the second century B.C. The silk route was in active use, and Palmyra benefited from it. Palmyrenes visited, and traded with, many Parthian cities: Hatra, Babylon, Seleucia, Spasinou Charax, and Susa.[15]

---

[10] H. Seyrig, "Ornamenta Palmyrena antiquiora," *Syria* 21 (1940), 277–328, and "Remarques sur la civilisation de Palmyre," ibid., 328–337.

[11] See below, note 38.   [12] Seyrig, *Syria* 21 (1940), 334.

[13] F. Cumont, *Fouilles de Doura-Europos (1922–1923)*, Bibliothèque archéologique et historique, IX (Paris: Paul Geuthner, 1926), pp. 29–41; in pages 41–136 the author has studied the mural paintings of the temple. For an outstanding synthesis of all the nuances involved in the origin and expansion of Greco-Parthian art, see D. Schlumberger, *L'Orient hellénisé: L'art grec et ses héritiers* . . . (Paris: Éditions Albin Michel, 1970); for its manifestation at Dura-Europos, see Cumont, *Doura-Europos (1922–1923)*, pp. 99–111.

[14] M.A.R. Colledge, *The Parthians* (New York: Frederick A. Praeger, 1967), pp. 77–78.

[15] Ibid., pp. 80–81. R. Ghirshman (*Iran* [Baltimore: Penguin Books, 1961], pp. 260–261, 283–284, 336, 342) and J. G. Février (*Essai sur l'histoire politique et économique de Palmyre* [Paris: Librairie philosophique J. Vrin, 1931], pp. 50–57, 72–73) offer a general view of the commercial relations linking Mesopotamia to Central Asia and the Far

Palmyra had a well-organized system of caravans with a local army in charge of the defense of the trade routes along the desert. This situation did not change once Rome seized the city. As a matter of fact the great number of statues and public buildings erected under the Romans show that the commercial activity of Palmyra increased.

At the beginning of our era—November, 21—the important tribes of the Bene Komare and the Bene Mattabol erected a statue to Hashash son of Nesa, a prominent member of the Bene Komare, because "he stood up at their head and made peace between them."[16] These tribes were two of the four which formed the nucleus of the earliest Palmyra. A bilingual inscription of August, 81 mentions the name of the third tribe, the Bene Maazin, whose name is rendered in Greek by the term "Palmyrene."[17] The identity of the terms "Bene Maazin" and "Palmyrene" accepted by the text is relevant indeed. We do not know the name

---

East. On the silk at Palmyra, see the studies of R. Pfister, *Textiles de Palmyre* (Paris: Éditions d'art et d'histoire, 1934), and *Nouveaux textiles de Palmyre* (ibid., 1937), and the remarks of H. Seyrig in *Syria* 22 (1941) 262–263; also N. Pigulevskaja, *Les villes de l'état Iranian aux époques parthe et sassanide*, École pratique des Hautes Études, Documents et recherches, vi (Paris: Mouton, 1963), pp. 163–169. Firsthand information about Palmyrene trade is found in the honorary inscriptions of the agora of Palmyra; see *Inventaire des inscriptions de Palmyre*, x, ed. J. Starcky (Damascus, 1949). The texts cover the period from 30 or 31 to 218 of our era. They were written on the consoles of the columns of the marketplace below the statues of persons honored by the city. This privilege was granted by the senate (*bwl'*) and people (*dms*) of Palmyra to the promoters of international trade.

[16] G. A. Cooke, *A Text-Book of North-Semitic Inscriptions* (Oxford: Clarendon Press, 1903), p. 293, no. 132.

[17] *Inventaire*, x, ed. Starcky, no. 40, and D. Schlumberger, "Les quatre tribus de Palmyre," *Syria* 48 (1971), 121–133, especially p. 126. The thesis, defended by Milik (*Dédicaces*, p. 30) and Gawlikowski (*Le temple palmyrénien*, p. 47), that the concept of the four tribes is an artificial creation of Roman Palmyra seems to me to be gratuitous. The presence of the four sanctuaries at Palmyra (see following note), one for each tribe, cannot be disparaged.

of the fourth tribe, but the existence of four different sanctuaries, each one the property of a tribe, is a fact well supported by the inscriptions. The four sanctuaries were dedicated to Baal Shamin, to Aglibol and Malakbel, to Arṣu, and to Atargatis.[18]

Palmyra was first governed by an assembly, "the assembly of all Palmyrenes,"[19] in which, it seems, the members of all the tribes were entitled to take part. Later on, in the second part of the first century of our era, and under Roman influence, a senate was substituted for the assembly. The hegemony of a few tribes, for instance, of the four mentioned above, was, of course, compatible with the presence of a local senate at which Rome was represented by a legate. The Tariff of Palmyra mentions the existence of this *hygmwn'*, in Greek *hegemon*, who presided over all kinds of contracts and imposed the fiscal law upon the city according to the rule that obtained in Syria.[20] But there was another Roman representative at Palmyra, called by the

[18] Gawlikowski, *Le temple palmyrénien*, pp. 48–52. According to a newly found bilingual text (Dunant, *Les inscriptions*, pp. 56–58, no. 45), the god Arṣu of Palmyra is Ares, whose cult enjoyed the favor of the Edessenes; cf. Julian *Orationes* 4. 150CD and 154B, who says that they adored the Sun flanked by Azizos (Ares) and Monimos (Hermes). Julian's text seems to be a reference to the planets Venus and Mercury, but scholars differ in their understanding of this passage; see H.J.W. Drijvers, "The Cult of Azizos and Monimos at Edessa" in *Ex Orbe religionum* [Festschrift G. Widengren] (Leiden: E. J. Brill, 1972), pp. 355–371, and J. Starcky, "Relief dédié au dieu Mun'im," in *Semitica* 22 (1972), 62–63. Cf. ch. Three, note 61.

[19] *Inventaire des inscriptions de Palmyre*, IX, ed. J. Cantineau (Damascus, 1933); in no. 8, the Palmyrene text says: *gbl tdmry' klhn*, whereas the Greek counterpart has "the city (*polis*) of the Palmyrenes"; in no. 12, Palm.: *gbl tdmry'*, and Greek: "the people (*dēmos*) of the Palmyrenes."

[20] The Tariff dates to A.D. 137. It was found in 1882, and in 1901 was taken into the Hermitage Museum. It measures 8.80 m by 1.75 m, and contains more than four hundred lines of Greek and Palmyrene text. For the inscription, see *CISem.*, II, 3913, lines 1–13 (Greek) and lines 1–11 (Palm.). The most important study published so far is that of H. Seyrig in *Syria* 22 (1941), 155–174.

Greek texts the *tetagmenos*. This term ought to be interpreted as meaning not "prefect" but "military officer."[21]

In 129 Hadrian visited Palmyra and gave her a new status: *civitas libera*. A decree of 137 included in the fiscal law shows that the senate of Palmyra was independent by then and Rome no longer controlled the payment of taxes.

Around 215 Caracalla gave Palmyra the status of *colonia*. This represented the peak of her glory. In 241, at the time of Shapur's struggle against Rome, Palmyra under her ruler Odenathus became a fervent defender of Rome in the Near Eastern provinces and an important factor in Roman policy for the area. Odenathus was granted the title *dux Romanorum* by Gallienus, and after his victory over Persia, that of *imperator*. Exceptional circumstances justified even the concession of the title *corrector totius Orientis*. Odenathus enlarged his territory up to the Taurus Mountains in the north and down to the Persian Gulf in the south. In 267 or 268, Odenathus was assassinated, and Palmyra entered a new era of political upheaval under Zenobia, the wife of the dead monarch.

The important part that Palmyrene soldiers played in the Roman army for many years must have heightened in them a consciousness of their worth for Palmyra and her allies while promoting a new desire for independence. On the other hand, the German invasions of Italy probably fostered the conviction among Palmyrenes that Rome was no longer able to hold the reins in the East. This was when Zenobia chose to break the links with Rome. In 271 she gave Wahballat, her son, the title *Augustus*. Zenobia reopened the mint of Antioch and struck coins representing Wahballat. Aurelian's reaction was swift. In the summer of 271 he marched overland to the East through the Balkans and defeated the Palmyrenes twice, in 272 and in 273. Palmyra survived the defeat, but never recovered; the city became nothing but a halt in the *strata diocletiana*, the route linking Damascus to the Euphrates.

21 Ibid., p. 159.

The Ancestral God Yarhibol and the Spring of Efca

The importance of springs as centers of settled life in ancient times is well documented in archaeology. At Palmyra the spring of Efca was very likely the first inhabited area of the oasis, but it is impossible to know at present when the first settlers arrived there, for the spring itself has not yet been excavated.[22] Nomads and settlers considered the spring to be under the special protection of a god, and inscriptions of all times show that the god Yarhibol took care of it. The name of the spring is mentioned in only two inscriptions,[23] but the name of the god and his relation to the spring appear quite often in inscriptions. At Dura-Europos, the military town that lay on the Middle Euphrates,[24] the Palmyrene archers of the tribe of the Bene Mitha invoked Yarhibol as "the idol of the spring" (*mṣb' dy 'yn'*).[25] This inscription clearly indicates that one of the

[22] The clearing operation of 1947 and 1948 (see Dj. al-Hassani and J. Starcky, "Autels palmyréniens découverts près de la source Efca," *Annales archéologiques de Syrie* 7 [1957], 115–122) and the exploratory visit of R. du Mesnil du Buisson in 1965 (see his report, cited in note 4 above, pp. 160–162) are, of course, insufficient to establish the date of the first settlement.

[23] Al-Hassani and Starcky, *Annales archéologiques de Syrie* 7 (1957), 101–111, nos. A1167–1168, and M. Gawlikowski, *Recueil d'inscriptions palmyréniennes provenant des fouilles syriennes et polonaises récentes à Palmyre* (hereafter *Inscriptions palmyréniennes*) (Paris: Imprimerie Nationale, C. Klincksieck, 1974), pp. 60–61, nos. 125–126.

[24] See D. Schlumberger, *Gnomon* 11 (1935), 87–93. Schlumberger rightly denies Dura the title "caravan city" given to her by M. I. Rostovtzeff in *Caravan Cities* (Oxford: Clarendon Press, 1932).

[25] C. C. Torrey in M. I. Rostovtzeff, F. E. Brown, and C. B. Welles, eds., *The Excavations at Dura-Europos: Preliminary Report of the Seventh and Eighth Seasons of Work, 1933–1934 and 1934–1935* (hereafter *Dura-Europos: Preliminary Report*) (New Haven: Yale University Press, 1939), pp. 279–281, and R. du Mesnil du Buisson, *Inventaire des inscriptions palmyréniennes de Doura-Europos* (Paris: Paul Geuthner, 1939), p. 18, no. 33. A relief cut from a rectangular slab of gypsum half a meter high represents Yarhibol in military dress, standing with his right hand raised to grasp his lance and his left hand gripping the hilt of a sword. He wears a short tunic and ample paludamentum, and his head is radiate; see F. E. Brown, *Dura-Europos: Preliminary Report*, pp. 264–265, pl. xxxv, 2.

prerogatives for which the god was known was the patron-
age he exercised over the spring of Efca. The interpretation
of the term *mṣb'*, "idol," is confirmed by two inscriptions
which mention "the priest of the idol of the spring."[26] Moreover, an altar was erected to Yarhibol by a certain Bolana
son of Azizu, who styled the god as the *gad*, i.e., "the patron," of the blessed spring.[27]

The texts invite us to see in the divine name Yarhibol an
allusion to the role that the god played at the spring according to the beliefs of the first inhabitants of the area,
who were of Amorite extraction. The name Yarhibol is
currently interpreted as meaning "the moon of Bol." This
title, however, does not fit the function performed by the
god in the pantheon of Palmyra. In fact, as we will see, he
represents the Sun god when he is associated with Bel,
the supreme deity of the city. Thus, the element *yarḥ* should
not be related to the common Semitic root *yrḥ*, which means
"moon" or "month." Perhaps *yarḥ* designated a "watering
place," "spring," or the like,[28] and the divine name describes
the relation of the god to the site.

Yarhibol, as the patron of the spring, appointed its "su-
perintendents," *epimelētēs* in Greek and *rb 'yn* in Palmy-

[26] *'pkl' dy mṣb 'yn'*; see *CISem.*, II, 4064, 4065. A distinction between
the terms *apkalla* and *kmr'*, "priest," at Palmyra cannot be established
yet. The first is attested among the Nabataeans and at Hatra; see J.
Teixidor, "Notes hatréennes," *Syria* 43 (1966), 91–93, and Gawlikowski,
Le temple palmyrénien (cited in note 4 above), p. 112.

[27] *CISem.*, II, 3976. Milik, *Dédicaces*, p. 165, does not seem to accept
the identification of Gad with Yarhibol, but the wording of the dedicatory formula supports my translation.

[28] J. Lewy, *Hebrew Union College Annual* 19 (1945–1946), 431, note
139, says that *yarḫu* is of Hurrian origin, and was used in Akkadian to
designate a "fountain" or a "watering place." The meaning of *Yarhibol*
would then be "the Lord who acts in the well" or the like. On the origin
of the word, see Kupper (cited in note 2 above), p. 71, note 3. H. B.
Huffmon lists the origin of the root *yrḥ* as uncertain: see his *Amorite
Personal Names in the Mari Texts* (Baltimore: Johns Hopkins University Press, 1965), p. 214. For *jarḫu*, "water hole, pond," in the Akkadian
texts, see *The Assyrian Dictionary*, Oriental Institute of the University
of Chicago (Chicago: University of Chicago Press, 1956–), vol. 7 (1960),
p. 325.

rene;[29] but the functions of the god transcended the confined territory of the spring to such an extent that some texts present Yarhibol as playing an important part in the official life of Palmyra. Yarhibol, for instance, bore witness for some individuals, attested oaths,[30] or allotted lands or villages to particular gods, whom he placed in charge of the inhabitants. A text from Khirbet Semrin, in the Palmyrene region, reads: "Let Abgal, his brothers, and the members of his house be remembered to Yarhibol, who gave [the god] Abgal authority over [this] locality. Let whoever fears [the god] Abgal be remembered!"[31] Abgal was a genie of the desert, the patron of cameleers and Bedouin in the Palmyrene steppe.[32]

Yarhibol exercised his authority over the life of the city by means of oracles. Some texts say that the god "chose" ('ḥd) his protégés; the correct interpretation of the term 'ḥd, however, is "to seize." It connotes the "taking hold" of somebody or something violently;[33] the verb 'ḥd ('ḥz) can even indicate the act of conquering a city, as in the inscription of Mesha, king of Moab, in the ninth century B.C.[34] Seizure of their chosen by the gods is by no means

[29] Gawlikowski, *Inscriptions palmyréniennes*, p. 60, no. 125.

[30] See, for instance, Cooke, *North-Semitic Inscriptions*, pp. 278–279, no. 121 (*CISem.*, II, 3932); J. Cantineau, "Tadmorea," *Syria* 17 (1936), 353–354, no. 26, line 9, with corrections, not always acceptable, of Milik in *Dédicaces*, pp. 300–303.

[31] Gawlikowski, *Le temple palmyrénien*, pp. 114–115, rightly states that Abgal is a god or genie, not an individual from the locality as H. Ingholt and J. Starcky assert in D. Schlumberger, *La Palmyrène du Nord-Ouest*, Bibliothèque archéologique et historique, XLIX (Paris: Paul Geuthner, 1951), p. 144.

[32] See H. Ingholt, *Studier over Palmyrensk Skulptur* (Copenhagen: Reitzel, 1928), pl. VII, 1; H. Seyrig, "Les dieux armés et les Arabes en Syrie," *Syria* 47 (1970), 79–87. Abgal had a temple at Khirbet Semrin on top of Ğebel Saar (1,250 m. high), which was excavated by D. Schlumberger in 1934–1935; see his *La Palmyrène du Nord-Ouest*, pp. 14–22, 55, pl. XXI, 1, 2.

[33] See *Inventaire des inscriptions de Palmyre*, XII, ed. A. Bounni and J. Teixidor (Beirut, 1976), no. 44.

[34] See *KAI* 181, line 11: *w'ltḥm bqr w'ḥzh*, "and I fought against the city, and I took it."

an unknown event in ancient Near Eastern literature or in the epigraphical texts.[35]

The cult of Yarhibol as the patron of the spring of Efca must have been very ancient for the god to have had the right to interfere in the life of Palmyra. This conclusion is also to be drawn from the very name *Yarhibol*, in which the ancient form *bol* is preserved. *Bol* was most probably the local rendering of the Canaanite-Phoenician *Baal*, a term which came to mean "lord" and was usually employed to designate the god of a locality.

However important the cult of Yarhibol may have been in the vicinity of the spring of Efca, Bel enjoyed the first rank and was for all purposes the supreme deity of the pantheon. His cult may have come to Palmyra with the northwestern tribes that, before moving toward the Syrian Desert, shared the Canaanite culture with the people of the Mediterranean coast.

BEL AND HIS TEMPLE

The official god *Bol* of pre-Hellenistic Palmyra probably had his name changed into that of *Bel* under the influence of the Mesopotamian cult of Bel Marduk, the chief god in the Babylonian pantheon. This change, however, must have taken place at a late date, for the element *bol* has remained in many Palmyrene personal names, for instance, Zabdibol ("Gift of Bol"), Borropha ("Bol has healed"), Gaddibol ("Bol is patron"), etc. A reference point for the shift Bol/Bel can be found in 217 B.C., at the battle of Raphia. We know that among the troops of Antiochus III in that engagement there was an Arab chieftain named Zabdibel ("Gift of Bel").[36] The name being unknown outside Palmyra, it seems legitimate to conclude that Zabdibel was a Palmyrene whose name mirrored already the new pronunciation of the name of the Palmyrene god.

The Palmyrene inscriptions inform us of the association

[35] See pp. 58–59.   [36] See above, note 6.

of Yarhibol with Bel and Aglibol in the cult which was performed at the main temple of the city. The temple, still standing today, was dedicated in A.D. 32. The following inscription, found in 1932, makes an interesting reference to the event: "In the month Tishri, the year 357 [October, A.D. 45]. This is the statue of Lishamsh son of Taibbol son of Shokaibel, of [the tribe of] the Bene Komare, who dedicated the temple (dy ḥnk hykl) of Bel, Yarhibol, and Aglibol, the gods ('lhy'), the day of their feast (bqdšwhy), the sixth day of Nisan, year 343 [April 6, 32]. His children erected the statue in his honor."[37]

The temple of 32 succeeded an old sanctuary the remains of which were buried under the huge platform created for the new temple. The cella and peristyle were elevated on a podium which is reached by a flight of steps on the western side. Here a sumptuous portal gives access to the interior of the cella. Archaeological excavations in the center of the temple court have uncovered an ancient wall some of whose stones bear inscriptions. They are among the earliest Palmyrene texts, to be dated in the first century B.C. On one of them is an inscription which reads as follows: "In the month Tishri, the year 269 [October, 44 B.C.], the priests of Bel erected this statue to Goraimai son of Nebuzabad, of the tribe of the Bene Kohenebol."[38] The remarkable difference between this text and that of A.D. 32 is that each mentions a different type of cult. In 44 B.C. Bel was worshiped alone in his temple,[39] whereas in A.D. 32 he had associated himself with two major gods of the city. A text of 33 B.C. found at Dura-Europos seems to provide us with

---

[37] Inventaire, IX, ed. Cantineau, no. 1, and Gawlikowski, Le temple palmyrénien, p. 68, no. 1.

[38] Inventaire des inscriptions de Palmyre, XI, ed. J. Teixidor (Beirut, 1965), no. 100; Milik, Dédicaces, p. 31.

[39] At this time Yarhibol had his own sanctuary; see J. Cantineau, Syria 17 (1936), 350–352, no. 25. Line 11 includes the phrase dwr' dy yrḥbwl, "the enclosure of Yarhibol," which means that the god had a precinct consecrated to him alone; see Milik, Dédicaces, pp. 303–304, and Gawlikowski, Le temple palmyrénien, pp. 56–57, 78–79. This "enclosure" of Yarhibol was probably his temple at the spring of Efca.

information regarding the intermediate stage of that cultic development. The inscription says: "In the month Sivan, the year 279, Zabdibol son of *b'yḥw*, of the [tribe of the] Bene Gaddibol, and Maliku son of Rumu, of the [tribe of the] Bene Komare, made the shrine for Bel and Yarhibol."[40]

Thus, the series of texts of the years 44 B.C., 33 B.C., and A.D. 32 show that the theological convictions of the Palmyrenes developed in a way that led to the acceptance of a trinity of gods. This probably happened under Babylonian influence, which tended to arrange deities in groups. The Palmyrene trinity bears no similarity to the one encountered in the Phoenician pantheons. By their theological speculation the Palmyrenes intended to assemble only the ancient powers of their religious life: Yarhibol, the god of the spring of Efca; Bel, whose cult must have come from the Canaanite coast in early days;[41] and Aglibol, whose character of North Syrian god seems undisputed.[42] In this trinity Yarhibol represents the Sun god and Aglibol the Moon god, whereupon the trinity conveys the belief in a cosmic order according to which Sun and Moon are portrayed as the acolytes of Bel, who is called Zeus by the Greek texts of Palmyra.

We know little about Bel and his sanctuary before A.D. 32, i.e., before the time when the priests of Bel elaborated

---

[40] Du Mesnil du Buisson, *Inscriptions palmyréniennes de Doura-Europos* (as cited in note 25 above), no. 1.

[41] Some Phoenician elements in the vocabulary and in the Palmyrene grammar certainly point to an influence of the coast over the oasis.

[42] The element *'gl* in Aglibol may derive from a root meaning "to roll," which would lead us to interpret the name as "the cart of Bol" and to relate it to the title *Rakib-El*, "the charioteer of El," borne by the Moon god at Ya'udi in the eighth century B.C. (*KAI* 24; 214). The preeminence of the Moon god over the Sun god is apparent in North Syrian inscriptions of the eighth and seventh centuries B.C. At Palmyra, monuments and inscriptions indicate that Aglibol excelled Malakbel, who became the *sol sanctissimus* of the Palmyrenes living in Rome in the third century of our era (*CISem.*, II, 3903).

a new theological system presenting Bel as a supreme god accompanied by two acolytes, the Sun and the Moon, thus making him a cosmic deity. Some inscriptions among the ruins of the first temple of Bel mention the names of the gods of various tribal factions. Their cult must have shared with that of Bel in the sacred area. They were: Manawat, an Arabian goddess;[43] Herta and Nanai, Babylonian deities; Aglibol; Reshef, a Canaanite god who was later identified with Apollo; Bol'astar and the demons (*šdy'*); Baaltak, a goddess whose cult was associated with that of Bel; she was most probably the consort of Bel, her surname (*Baaltak*, "Your Lady") deriving from a liturgical invocation.[44] All these deities were venerated in the area in which Bel had his temple. The Palmyrenes in fact called this temple "the house of the gods."[45] In this expression a remnant of the assemblies of the gods in the Canaanite and Phoenician pantheons can be seen. The gods were invoked by the faith-

[43] The correct pronunciation, according to the Nabataean inscriptions, seems to be *Manotu*. Her cult is profusely attested among Nabataeans, Palmyrenes, and Arabs. The name means "destiny," "fate." See the studies of Starcky, *Suppl. DB*, VII, cols. 1000–1001; A. Grohman, *Kulturgeschichte des Alten Orients: Arabien* (Munich: C. H. Beck, 1963), pp. 82, 84, and M. Höfner in *Götter und Mythen im Vorderen Orient*, ed. H. W. Haussig (Stuttgart: Ernst Klett, 1965), pp. 454–455.

[44] Gawlikowski, *Le temple palmyrénien*, pp. 33–34, and Milik, *Dédicaces*, p. 174. The number of female deities mentioned by the Palmyrene inscriptions is high indeed. Most probably this means that the same deity was invoked under different names. In the case of Allat my conjecture is that the names Astarte-Ishtar, *b'ltk*, Belti, *gd dy ydy'bl*, refer to her. Names presumably changed according to the various ethnic groups and their religious background: Aramaean, Phoenician, Arab, Babylonian, etc. In the Arab temple of the western quarter of the city the goddess is consistently invoked as Allat or as the "Lady of the temple." M. Gawlikowski has published some of the archaeological evidence concerning this temple in "Allat et Baalshamin," *Mélanges d'histoire ancienne et d'archéologie offerts à Paul Collart*, Cahiers d'archéologie romande, no. 5 (Lausanne and Paris: De Boccard, 1976), pp. 197–203.

[45] Gawlikowski, *Le temple palmyrénien*, pp. 56–64, where the author has collected the various texts belonging to the period of the first temple.

ful as "the sons of god," "the great council of all the saints,"
"the whole family of the children of the gods," "the whole
assembly of the holy gods."[46] The Palmyrene term "the
house of the gods," together with some philological facts
found in the inscriptions, seems to indicate that the cult
of Bel and of the family of the gods at Palmyra is to be
traced back to the years in which the founders of Palmyra
had been under the influence of Phoenician culture.

Future archaeological research is unlikely to clarify the
structure of the first temple of Bel, for the ancient architects leveled the area when the new sanctuary was erected.
This coincides with the time when the Palmyrene citizens
engaged themselves in the construction of numerous public
buildings. The temple, however, remains the best example
of that feverish activity. The new cella presumably preserved the structure of the ancient one in an enlarged and
more ornamented manner.[47] The court of the temple was
decorated with statues of prominent citizens; we know, for
instance, that a statue was erected to Yedibel son of Azizo
by the Palmyrene merchants and the Greek businessmen
of Seleucia, who thanked him for his leadership and his
generous contribution to the construction of the temple.[48]
A statue was also erected to Hashash son of Nesa in A.D. 21
because "he established peace between the Bene Komare
and the Bene Mattabol, and he himself supervised all the
details of the agreement."[49] In A.D. 25 the treasurers of the
temple and the assembly of the city erected another statue
to Maliku, a brother of Hashash to thank him for his gen-
erosity in helping in the construction of the temple, "the
house of the gods";[50] the year before, the merchants had

[46] See Ch. One, note 30.

[47] Nothing, of course, is known about the ancient cella, but the articles of H. Seyrig in *Syria* 21 (1940), 277–337, and 22 (1941), 31–44,
are of great help to the historian of Palmyra for the period before A.D.
32; see also Gawlikowski, *Le temple palmyrénien*, pp. 65–66.

[48] *Inventaire*, IX, ed. Cantineau, no. 6a.

[49] Ibid., no. 13 (Cooke, *North-Semitic Inscriptions*, no. 132).

[50] *Inventaire*, IX, ed. Cantineau, no. 12a.

erected a statue to him for the same reason, but in this inscription the donors wanted to emphasize that Maliku's contribution had been the most generous ever.[51] In A.D. 51 an inscription on the statue of Moqimu son of Ogeilu, nicknamed Hokkaisu, states that the assembly of Palmyra honored him because of the various gifts he made to the temple. The Greek part of the inscription, completing the Palmyrene one, indicates that Moqimu offered a vase for libations, a gold altar worth 150 dinars, four golden bowls worth 120 dinars, and a pillow for the couch of the shrine.[52]

The worship of Bel, Yarhibol, and Aglibol together as practiced in the main temple of Palmyra does not constitute an isolated form of cult among the religious mores of the ancient Near East. Phoenician inscriptions, for instance, often record cultic acts performed in honor of Melqart, the Tyrian god, and Eshmun, his divine counterpart at Sidon; several inscriptions from Kition report such an association of deities.[53] Another example can be found in the cult of Astarte and Tenit at Sarepta in Phoenicia.[54] A gold pendant

[51] Ibid., no. 11.

[52] Ibid., no. 8; Milik, *Dédicaces*, pp. 154–155; and Gawlikowski, *Le temple palmyrénien*, pp. 69–70. A citizen's contribution of money to the building of the temple was not always the reason for the dedication of a statue to him in the temple court; sometimes citizens were honored either by the senate or by individuals for reasons now unknown.

[53] See M. G. Guzzo Amadasi in *Rivista di studi fenici* 1 (1973), 133; Teixidor, BES 1974, no. 118.

[54] The two names appear in a Phoenician inscription written on a small plaque of ivory found by James B. Pritchard in his excavations. Dr. Pritchard granted me permission to examine the object in the Beirut Museum. The association of female deities is a Hellenistic phenomenon, but it is difficult to be certain of the religious intentions of the faithful; at Delos, for instance, the Orientals worshiped Aphrodite-Astarte, Aphrodite-Atargatis, Aphrodite *and* Isis; see P. Bruneau, *Recherches sur les cultes de Délos à l'époque hellénistique et à l'époque impériale* (Paris: E. de Boccard, 1970), pp. 346–347. A Phoenician in-

from Carthage, to be dated about 700 B.C., is dedicated to Astarte and Pygmalion.[55] Among the inscriptions recently found at Antas, in Sardinia, at least one mentions the offering of a statue of the god Šadrafa to Ṣid, the supreme deity of the area.[56] A Greek inscription of A.D. 224 from Jebel Siman, in North Syria, records the construction of the oil mill of the temple dedicated to the local gods "Name," Symbetylos, and Lion.[57]

The theological implications of these associations cannot be easily grasped, but it seems certain that the faithful, in their daily devotions, felt the urge to bring together the supernatural powers rather than to leave them dispersed. The extant epigraphical material, Phoenician or Aramaic, does not support the conclusion that two or more gods, when worshiped together, had their personalities merged into one: the associations of deities were cultic and not the result of metaphysical considerations. But, on the other hand, the inscriptions do not portray Phoenician or Aramaean religion as a phenomenon of atomization either. The frequent associations of gods recorded in the inscriptions clearly reveal that a simple act of faith could embrace the various aspects under which the devotee had conceived the divine. Of course, the god was always the patron deity of

---

scription from Memphis also makes a clear distinction between Isis and Astarte; see *KAI* 48. This is likewise the case in a Greek text from Palmyra; see Milik, *Dédicaces*, p. 54, and Teixidor, BES 1968, no. 26. The distinction, however, is deliberately denied in book 11 of Apuleius's *Metamorphoses*, where *Venus* and *Isis* are two names of *Regina caeli*.

[55] See J. B. Peckham, *The Development of the Late Phoenician Scripts* (Cambridge, Mass.: Harvard University Press, 1968), pp. 119–123.

[56] M. Fantar in E. Acquaro et al., *Ricerche puniche ad Antas*, Studi semitici, no. 30 (Rome: Istituto di studi del Vicino Oriente, 1969), pp. 79–81. Three inscriptions from Carthage mention individuals who were "servants of the temple of Ṣid-Tenit" there: *CISem.*, I, 247–249.

[57] W. K. Prentice, *Greek and Latin Inscriptions: Northern Syria*, Publications of the Princeton University Archaeological Expeditions to Syria in 1904–1905 and 1909, div. III, sect. B (Leiden: E. J. Brill, 1922), pp. 180–185, no. 1170, and J. T. Milik, *Biblica* 48 (1967), 568–569.

a family, of a tribe, or of an ethnic group, and the association of two or more gods could at times have been the result of a political move supported by two or more friendly groups or even by two or more rivals faced by a common enemy. The simplest and most effective manner of securing the support of an ally, or of defeating an enemy, was to secure the favor of his gods. This is what the Roman historians refer to as the practice of *evocatio*, namely, the calling out of the gods from a besieged city, officially inviting them to form part of the pantheon of the besieger.[58]

The reasons that might have motivated the priests of Bel to incorporate Yarhibol's cult into that performed in the temple of Bel can be ascertained. Yarhibol's cult was ancient and well established, and its absorption by the main sanctuary of the city indicates that the cult of Bel needed the universal support of all the inhabitants, especially if, as seems to have been the case, each god was the patron of a specific group. The same "political" move can be detected in the official incorporation of the cult of Aglibol into the main temple. Aglibol is mentioned in an inscription of 17 B.C., and it seems that he and his companion, Malakbel, by then were worshiped by the tribe of the Komare (initially the Bene Kohenite) in a sanctuary known as "the holy garden."[59] The Palmyrene term used for "holy garden" in the bilingual inscription of A.D. 132 is *gnt' 'lym*.[60] Both

[58] V. Basanoff, *Evocatio: Étude d'un rituel militaire romain*, Bibliothèque de l'École des Hautes Études, Sciences religieuses, LXI (Paris, 1947). The *carmen evocationis* is known from Macrobius *Saturnalia* 3. 9.

[59] See Milik, *Dédicaces*, p. 62; Gawlikowski, *Le temple palmyrénien*, p. 50.

[60] Dunant, *Les inscriptions* (cited in note 4 above), pp. 56–59, no. 45, line 12. The sanctuary of the two gods has not yet been found, but it is represented on a tessera; see H. Ingholt et al., *Recueil des tessères de Palmyre* (Paris: Paul Geuthner, 1955), p. 23, no. 162, and on a frieze in

the initial name of the tribe in charge of the sanctuary, the Bene Kohenite—from Phoenician *kohen*, "priest"—and the word *'lym*, literally meaning "the gods" or "holy" in Phoenician, show that the tribe was an ancient Canaanite group which had become well established in Palmyra by A.D. 32, i.e., the time when the temple of Bel was dedicated. The "holy garden" of Aglibol and Malakbel must have been one of the earliest temples of Palmyra. Its importance is underlined by the inscription of A.D. 132 in which the sanctuaries of the four founding tribes of Palmyra are mentioned. Aglibol, a Moon god, and Malakbel, a vegetation god, were known in the texts as the "Holy Brothers," and so they are represented on a frieze in the peristyle of the temple of Bel in the act of shaking hands.[61]

In spite of the official grouping of the three gods Bel, Yarhibol, and Aglibol in the cult of the main temple, inscriptions of all periods show that Yarhibol never lost his leading role in the organization of the civil life of Palmyra, which means that, in spite of his association with Bel the god of the spring did not decline in rank in the minds of the citizens. His privileged position of ancestral god was always acknowledged, and his responsibilities in the civic life of the city never diminished. This is indeed noticeable even in late inscriptions.[62]

---

the temple of Bel; see H. Seyrig in *Syria* 15 (1934), 172–173, pl. XXII. Here the garden is symbolized by a palm tree and two altars with fruit, whereas on the tessera the sacred tree is a cypress, as in two reliefs in the Capitoline Museum at Rome; see H. Seyrig, *Syria* 48 (1971), 101–103.

[61] *Syria* 15 (1934), pl. XXII. This friendly gesture is also represented on a relief in the Capitoline Museum in Rome (for a good reproduction see *Syria* 18 [1937], pl. XXXI) and on another from Khirbet Ramadan, near Palmyra (see Schlumberger, *La Palmyrène du Nord-Ouest* [cited in note 31 above], pl. XXXVI, 1).

[62] Gawlikowski, *Inscriptions palmyréniennes* (cited in note 23 above), pp. 61–62, no. 127 (dated A.D. 205); *Inventaire*, XII, ed. Bounni and Teixidor (cited in note 33 above), no. 44 (dated A.D. 206); and *Inventaire des inscriptions de Palmyre*, III, ed. J. Cantineau (Damascus, 1930), no. 22 (A.D. 242–243).

THE "ANONYMOUS" GOD

Altars dedicated to "the one whose name is blessed for ever" have been found in the immediate surroundings of the spring of Efca.[63] It is surprising to find these expressions of faith in an "anonymous" god in a domain considered to be under Yarhibol's protection. But altars dedicated to the god "whose name is blessed for ever" have also been uncovered in other areas of Palmyra,[64] and the common view among scholars is that this "anonymous" god represents a late and spiritualized conception of Baal Shamin, "Lord of Heaven," whose temple still remains visible today. This conclusion, however, seems unsound. Except for an erratic example, no altars dedicated to "the one whose name is blessed for ever" have been found in the temple of Baal Shamin;[65] on the other hand, mention of the god "whose name is blessed for ever" occurs, among early instances, in an altar inscription of A.D. 128, i.e., three years before the temple of Baal Shamin was dedicated;[66] this altar was found at the foot of the Jebel Muntar, near the spring of Efca, and according to the text it was offered to the "anonymous" god by two gods, Belhamon and Manawat: a certain Ate'aqab son of Hairan represented the gods and paid the full price of the gift. Another altar inscription, dated in A.D. 132, namely, a year after the solemn dedication of the temple of Baal Shamin, appeared in the area known as the Camp of Diocletian.[67] It seems unlikely that

[63] Gawlikowski, *Inscriptions palmyréniennes*, nos. 106–127.

[64] See, for instance, ibid., nos. 129–130, 134–138, 140, 142, 144. G. A. Cooke has included a few of the inscriptions on the altars in *North-Semitic Inscriptions*, nos. 135, 137, 138. In *Inventaire*, XI, ed. Teixidor, nos. 1–10, 13–17, 19–20, 23–24, etc., the origin of some of the altars is unknown: they could well come from the area of the spring of Efca.

[65] P. Collart and J. Vicari, *Le sanctuaire de Baalshamin à Palmyre: Topographie et architecture* (hereafter *Architecture*), 2 vols. (Neuchâtel: P. Attinger, 1969), I, pp. 206 and 211.

[66] *Inventaire*, XII, ed. Bounni and Teixidor, no. 43.

[67] Gawlikowski, *Inscriptions palmyréniennes*, no. 130.

the cult of Baal Shamin, so profusely acclaimed around the year 130, had been in those very years the object of a devotion interested in concealing his cult under the ambiguous appellation "whose name is blessed for ever."

Scholars have tried to solve the question of the "anonymous" god's identity by equating the dedicatory formula "to the one whose name is blessed for ever" with formulae such as "to Zeus *hypsistos* and *epekoos*," "to the one, alone, and merciful god" or "to the Lord of the World," all of them present in Greek or Palmyrene inscriptions, on the ground that the name of the god to whom the offering was made is not mentioned in any of the formulae. But this is fallacious. The formulae "to Zeus *hypsistos* and *epekoos*" and "to the Lord of the World" suit Bel and Baal Shamin equally well; the phrase "to the one, sole, and merciful god" is no doubt addressed to Bel. This particular confession of monotheistic faith, written in Greek, appears in the court of the temple of Bel on an altar dedicated by Malkos son of Barea son of Malikos, who exercised the function of president of the senate about A.D. 200.[68] To be sure, Malkos was not a commoner, and the dedication, therefore, should not be overestimated. But, on the other hand, the inscription was in the court for anybody passing by to read and, presumably, understand.[69]

Thus, the formula "to the one whose name is blessed for ever" must be interpreted in a different context. It cannot conceal Baal Shamin's cult, for it would be paradoxical if a god adored in his sanctuary as Lord of Heaven should later have his name replaced by the formula "whose name

[68] *Inventaire*, x, ed. Starcky (cited in note 15 above), no. 55, and H. Seyrig, *Syria* 14 (1933), 269–275, and 22 (1941), 245–246.

[69] This is not an isolated instance. Many miles away, in the Maronite monastery of Deir el-Qala, on a sort of spur overlooking Beirut and among the ruins of a Roman building there was an altar dedicated in Greek to Baal Marqod, "the holy one god"; see Teixidor, BES 1972, no. 53. Baal Marqod was a Phoenician god adored by the people of the plain in his rustic chapel at the top of the mountain.

is blessed for ever," which leaves him in effect without a name. On the day the Temple of Jerusalem was consecrated Solomon said, among other things, "Will God indeed dwell on the earth? Behold heaven and the highest heaven cannot contain thee; how much less this house which I have built!" (1 Kings 8:27; also pertinent are verses 12 and 43). If his remarks that day are to have a meaning, the description of a supreme god as having the heavens for an abode might be expected to excel any other divine epithet.

To be sure, the Palmyrene devotion to the "anonymous" god ought not to be compared with that of the "unknown god" mentioned on the altar inscription of Athens, to whom Paul refers at the beginning of his speech on the Areopagus (Acts 17:22–23). Here Paul flatters his audience by saying that that particular form of cult shows the great solicitude of the Athenians for the worship of gods. In fact, the Athenian cult should be interpreted in the light of Acts 17:21: "All the Athenians and the foreigners who lived there spent their time in nothing except telling or hearing something new." A sure way of not missing anything new was to forecast it by dedicating an altar to the god yet to come to Athens. This epitomizes Athenian snobbism. At Palmyra, however, the cult of the "anonymous" god stemmed from an already existing cult; it was the result of a theological rationalization, negative as it may have been.

Some scholars tend to consider the cult of the "anonymous" god at Palmyra as the result of Jewish influence over the city, but the similarities that may exist between that particular form of Palmyrene religiosity and the monotheistic worship of Yahweh among the Jews are only apparent. The Jewish God of whom the Psalmist says: "Blessed be his glorious name for ever" (Psalm 72:19), had a name, as Exodus 3:14 records, but it was not pronounced, out of reverence. In the case of the "anonymous" god, the Palmyrenes knew the god they adored but opted for using a circumlocution when calling on him. But this could hardly have meant that that particular "unnamed" name was more blessed than other equally divine names of the Palmyrene pantheon. The evasive character of the circumlocution clearly points to a situation in which traditional forms of worship must have been reshaped in order to accommodate new people and new beliefs.

In the case of the Psalmist, or of Daniel (2:10), the historian can see an attitude consistent with the theology of the Old Testament, but in the cult of the "anonymous" god I see only a reflection of the skepticism professed by Celsus regarding divine names. In his book *Contra Celsum* Origen deals with the problem "whether, as Aristotle thinks, names were given by arbitrary determination; or, as the Stoics hold, by nature, the first utterances being imitations of the things described and becoming their names (in accordance with which they introduce certain etymological principles); or whether, as Epicurus teaches (his view not being the same as that held by the Stoics), names were given by nature, the first men having burst out with certain sounds descriptive of the objects."[70] Celsus states his views in a passage of remarkable interest: "The goatherds and shepherds thought that there was one God called the Most High, or Adonai, or the Heavenly One, or Sabaoth, or however they like to call this world; and they acknowledged nothing more. . . . It makes no difference whether one calls the supreme God by the name used among the Greeks, or by that, for example, used among the Indians, or by that among the Egyptians."[71]

Origen refuses to accept this principle. He believes that divine names were instituted in a consistent, albeit mys-

[70] Origen *Contra Celsum* 1. 24; trans. H. Chadwick (Cambridge: At the University Press, 1965), p. 23.

[71] Ibid. Of the word "world" Chadwick notes that the term is a reminiscence of Plato *Timaeus* 28B and that Jupiter may be called the world according to Seneca in *Naturales quaestiones* 2. 45. 3; see Chadwick, p. 23, note 3.

terious, way, and he quotes a passage from the *Philebus* of Plato to support his point.[72] This same text is cited by Julian in his *Orationes* 7 with the same purpose in mind: reverence for the names of the gods. Curiously enough, neither Origen nor Julian points to the sarcastic tone of Plato's passage. In Julian's words it reads as follows: "But for my part, Protarchus, I feel a more than human awe, indeed a fear beyond expression, of the names of the gods. Now therefore I will address Aphrodite by whatever name pleases her best; though as for pleasure, I know that it has many forms."[73]

It can be inferred from the many bilingual inscriptions which we possess that Palmyrenes as well as Phoenicians and Nabataeans would have accepted Celsus' statement that a deity could be worshiped under different names by different peoples. The Palmyrenes, to be sure, may not have shared the sarcastic views of the *Philebus*, but they certainly very often omitted the names of the gods in their dedications, using instead cultic circumlocutions such as "Lord of the World," the "Holy Brothers," or "Fortune of the Tribe." This practice is all the more surprising at Palmyra where the existence of a great number of deities could easily lead to confusion. Cultic formulae seem to have been as valid as the mention of a divine name. All this precludes the theory that the appearance of the formula "the one whose name is blessed for ever" indicates the religious evolution of Palmyra toward monotheism. This formula, far from being the result of deductive reasoning, is most probably a cultic invocation, one among others.

The Palmyrene inscriptions not only reflect the popular piety; they also inform us on the theological implications

[72] Origen *Contra Celsum* 1. 25; trans. Chadwick, pp. 25–26.
[73] Julian *Orationes* 7. 237A; I follow the translation and interpretation of W. C. Wright, Loeb Classical Library (Cambridge, Mass., 1969), II, p. 155.

of this piety. In the case of Yarhibol, of course, it is not easy to determine what happened to his cult at the spring of Efca once the god was officially installed in the main temple of the city to represent the Sun. It may be wondered whether the creation, first, of an official triad into which the main religious traditions of Palmyra were forced to merge and, later on, the increasing popularity of Baal Shamin, a supreme god of agriculture and settled life, did not shatter the religious traditions of the city so that the cult of Yarhibol acquired a new theological dimension.

In an inscription of A.D. 128, already mentioned, a citizen called Ateʻaqab paid for an altar to be dedicated by the gods Belhamon and Manawat to "the one whose name is blessed for ever." If the "anonymous" god meant here is Baal Shamin, it remains to be explained why the altar was offered in the vicinity of the spring of Efca and not in the precinct consecrated to Baal Shamin in the center of the city. The argument is equally valid should the "anonymous" god be considered a circumlocution to invoke Bel: it would have been improper for Belhamon and Manawat to dedicate an altar to Bel in this part of the city, between the spring of Efca and the jebel on top of which the two gods had their own sanctuaries,[74] rather than in Bel's own temple. The interpretation of the inscription of 128 becomes coherent if the god "whose name is blessed for ever" is Yarhibol. Gods dedicated altars and temples to one another, and this divine courtesy could have been extended to Yarhibol on behalf of Belhamon and Manawat. Belhamon, whose temple was built in May, A.D. 89, on top of the Jebel Muntar, exercised the functions of patron god of the tribe of the Bene Agrud. He was an avatar of Bel,[75] and as such

[74] See du Mesnil du Buisson (cited in note 4 above), pp. 165–174; *Inventaire*, XII, ed. Bounni and Teixidor, nos. 48–49.

[75] As proved by two inscriptions (*Inventaire*, XI, ed. Teixidor, no. 99, and Dessau, 4341, the latter a Latin inscription from Dacia studied by J. Starcky in "Inscriptions archaïques de Palmyre," *Studi orientalistici in onore di Giorgio Levi Della Vida*, II [Rome: Istituto per l'Oriente, 1956], pp. 517–518) and by a tessera (M. Gawlikowski, *Syria* 48 [1971],

his dedication of an altar to Yarhibol, the ancestral god, in the sacred area of the spring, becomes an altogether meaningful gesture.

The faithful, when offering altars to the god "whose name is blessed for ever," could have had in mind Yarhibol as the supreme Baal of the spring of Efca. Only if Yarhibol is the "anonymous" god can the great number of altars dedicated to the latter in the vicinity of the spring have a meaning. Few archaeological surveys have shown that there are ancient constructions around the spring. According to a text of A.D. 205 Bolha son of Hairan, the superintendent of the spring, paid for the erection of three walls that in some way formed part of the sacred pool.[76] As in our day, the spring must then have had its backwater.

The inscriptions fully document the fact that Yarhibol kept his autonomy in spite of having become a member of the official triad venerated at the temple of Bel. From texts of the years 162, 205,[77] and 206,[78] we know that Yarhibol appointed officials to take care of the spring and its surroundings. But some texts do not mention Yarhibol by name. A Greek inscription of the first part of the third century refers to "the ancestral god" (*theos patroos*) who gave his approval to the *strategos* Julius Aurelius Maliku son of Washu; the Palmyrene counterpart mentions "the god who bore witness" to the *strategos*.[79] A Palmyrene text of June, 193, also seems to omit the name of Yarhibol, who, according to the Greek section, gave his blessings to a

411–412). The origin of Belhamon's cult is uncertain. I believe that it came to Palmyra from Phoenicia; his cult is known at Zinjirli and in the western Punic colonies, and his name is to be interpreted as "Lord of the Amanus," the correct spelling therefore being Ḥamôn and not Ḥammôn; see F. M. Cross, *Canaanite Myth and Hebrew Epic* (Cambridge, Mass.: Harvard University Press, 1973), pp. 24–28.

[76] Gawlikowski, *Inscriptions palmyréniennes*, no. 127.

[77] Ibid., nos. 125 and 127.

[78] *Inventaire*, XII, ed. Bounni and Teixidor, no. 44.

[79] *Inventaire*, X, ed. Starcky, no. 115.

strategos and "chief of the market."[80] This kind of ano-
nymity suits Yarhibol, whose ancestral glory must have been
overwhelmed by the cult of Bel. It is easy to understand
that a formula such as the god "whose name is blessed for
ever" applies to Yarhibol better than to Bel or to Baal Shamin, whose names and prerogatives remained unchanged.
The periphrasis "whose name is blessed for ever" betrays
more the impact of a psychological experience than the
presence of a philosophical elucidation the end result of
which would be an act of monotheistic faith. The traditional view held by scholars that the cult of Baal Shamin
at Palmyra became that of the "anonymous" god as a con-
sequence of the enlightenment which the best minds of
the city enjoyed seems gratuitous. Offerings were made to
the "anonymous" god many years before a sumptuous temple was dedicated to Baal Shamin in the better quarters
of Palmyra. Moreover, the cult of Baal Shamin coexisted
with that offered to the "anonymous" god in the spring of
Efca as well as in the area where the temple of the Arab
gods stood.[81] It appears altogether incongruous that the
"enlightened" individuals of Palmyra professed their monotheistic faith in Baal Shamin by worshiping him in the
temples of other gods.

Because the formula "whose name is blessed for ever"
is cultic, it is loose enough to be applied to Yarhibol, a god
of ancestral rank, supreme master of the spring, but whose
cult may have lost its original form in the religious life of
the city. The formula could have been used occasionally
to designate other deities than Yarhibol, for instance, Bel
or Baal Shamin. This may explain the presence of altars
dedicated to the "anonymous" god all over the city. However, once his cult merged with that of Bel to become a
member of the official triad, Yarhibol, as a true Baal of the

---

[80] Ibid., no. 85; cf. Cooke, *North-Semitic Inscriptions*, no. 121.

[81] Gawlikowski, *Le temple palmyrénien* (cited in note 4 above), pp.
101–104, 108–110.

spring and the ancestral deity of the area, had more claims than any other deity to be referred to as the god "whose name is blessed for ever."

THE CULT OF BAAL SHAMIN AT PALMYRA

The temple of Baal Shamin is well known today after the excavations undertaken from 1954 to 1956 by Swiss archaeologists,[82] who uncovered most of its remains. The earliest inscription, found in the northern court of the sanctuary, is of November, 23 of our era. The text runs as follows: "In the month of Kanun, in the year 335, Attai and Shabhai, daughters of Shahra, and Atta, daughter of Firdus, have offered these two columns to Baal Shamin, the good god, for their lives and the lives of their children and brothers."[83]

Some thirty years later—in January, 52—another woman, Amtallat, daughter of Baraa, from the tribe of the Bene Mitha, wife of Taima son of Belhazai, from the tribe of the Bene Maazin, "dedicated a column to Baal Shamin, the good and bountiful god."[84] The tribes mentioned here are well known from other texts; the Bene Maazin, in particular, acquired preeminence in the temple of the god. Baal Shamin was their patron, and some of their members seem to have become at a certain moment the owners of the temple itself.[85]

The columns erected by these Palmyrene devotees must have been the earliest architectural elements of the monumental court, which was not officially consecrated until 67 of our era.[86] Prior to this there is, among other archaeological remains, an altar which a member of the Bene Maazin offered "to Baal Shamin, Durahlun, and Rahim, and

[82] Collart and Vicari, *Architecture* (cited in note 65 above), I (text) and II (plates).

[83] Dunant, *Les inscriptions* (cited in note 4 above), pp. 24–25, no. 10.

[84] Ibid., pp. 25–26, no. 11. [85] Ibid., pp. 10–11.

[86] Collart and Vicari, *Architecture*, I, pp. 43–45, 60–61.

to the Fortune of Yedibel" in A.D. 62.[87] The gods who here accompany Baal Shamin are tribal deities; one of them, Durahlun, is often associated with Baal Shamin in the inscriptions of the temple. He seems to have been the supreme god of the region of Rahle, on Mount Hermon.[88]

In 67 the entire area dedicated to the cult of Baal Shamin underwent great architectural activity. Several texts in the names of the donors of two of the porticoes of the northern court record the gifts.[89] The other two porticoes were paid for by various persons during a period that extended from

[87] Dunant, *Les inscriptions*, pp. 36–37, no. 23.

[88] See J. Starcky in Collart and Vicari, *Architecture*, I, pp. 216–217 (Milik, *Dédicaces*, p. 96, does not accept the association of Durahlun with Rahle). Collart (*Architecture*, I, pp. 179 and 217–218) has drawn attention to the architectural parallels existing at Palmyra and in the temples of Si'a, in the Hauran, and of Rahle on the slopes of Mount Hermon (the latter is described by D. Krencker and W. Zschietzschmann, *Römische Tempel in Syrien* [Berlin: W. de Gruyter, 1938], pp. 223–230 and pls. 94–97). These connections can be easily explained by the influence of Arab tribes who moved from the Anti-Lebanon or the Hauran to Palmyra. Therefore I am inclined to ascribe the cult of Baal Shamin at Palmyra to the Arab influence over the oasis (the Bene Maazin certainly were an Arab tribe): the importance of the Nabataean cult of Baal Shamin in the Hauran and the Phoenician influence over the Anti-Lebanon are no doubt elements of the cultural heritage borne by the migratory groups into Palmyra. (As far as the Phoenician influence over Rahle is concerned it should be recalled that in later times Rahle "was a see in the ecclesiastical province of Tyre and therefore probably a village of Sidon"; see A.H.M. Jones, *The Cities of the Eastern Roman Provinces*, 2nd ed. [Oxford: Clarendon Press, 1971], pp. 287 and 466, note 85.) The attraction that the Palmyrene oasis exerted upon the peripheral areas was no doubt due to the character of Palmyra as a caravan center. This historical phenomenon was to my view well exemplified in Castile during the fifteenth and sixteenth centuries when trade enabled the high plain to become the center of gravity of the Spanish peninsula; see, for instance, F. Braudel, *The Mediterranean and the Mediterranean World in the Age of Philip II*, I, trans. S. Reynolds from the French (New York: Harper and Row, 1972), p. 55.

[89] Collart and Vicari, *Architecture*, I, pp. 53–55.

67 to 103 or 104.[90] The usual formula by which the gifts were presented to the temple specifies that columns, architraves, and roofs "were offered to Baal Shamin and Duraḥlun, the good and bountiful gods."

Baal Shamin had the temple at the southern part of the main court.[91] This sanctuary, still standing today, is of Corinthian style; it was built in 131 according to the inscription, written in Greek and Palmyrene, which appears upon the bracket of a column that supported the bust of Male, a benefactor of the temple. Like many other honorary inscriptions visible on the columns that flank streets, courts, and porticoes, Male's inscription represents the tribute of the senate of Palmyra to an illustrious citizen. This inscription, however, is of particular interest because it makes a brief reference to the visit of the Emperor Hadrian to Palmyra around 129. The text reads as follows: "The Senate and the People have made this statue to Male Agrippa, son of Yarhai son of Lishamsh Raai, who, being secretary for a second time when the divine Hadrian came here, gave oil to the citizens, and to the troops and the strangers that came with him, taking care of their encampment. And he built the temple, the vestibule, and the entire decoration, at his own expense, to Baal Shamin and Duraḥlun."[92]

During the whole of the first century and the first decades of the second century altars were dedicated to Baal Shamin in a sacred area which had been provided with porticoes some time before the temple itself was erected.[93] One of

[90] Ibid., pp. 45, 60; Dunant, *Les inscriptions*, p. 29.

[91] Collart and Vicari, *Architecture*, I, pp. 190–198, think that the temple of Baal Shamin at Palmyra is a copy after that dedicated to the god at Si'a, in the Hauran.

[92] Instead of "Baal Shamin and Duraḥlun," the Greek text says only Zeus; see Dunant, *Les inscriptions*, pp. 55–56, no. 44. Milik, *Dédicaces*, p. 11, offers a different reading of line 6 in the Palmyrene text. After the emperor's visit Palmyra received the title *Hadriana Palmyra*; see Milik, ibid., p. 12, and J. Starcky, *Palmyre* (Paris: A. Maisonneuve, 1952), p. 38.

[93] Collart and Vicari, *Architecture*, I, pp. 65–66.

the altars, still standing on a large platform in front of the sanctuary, bears a bilingual inscription dated the seventh day of Shebat (the Greek month of Peritios) of 426, namely, February 7, 115. In this text the Greek dedication "to Zeus Most High and the one who listens to prayers" is rendered by the Palmyrene expression "to the Lord of the World" (*mare 'alma*; it can also be translated by "Lord of Eternity"). The offering was made by four brothers, Auida, Malku, Yarhibola, and Hagegu, the children of Bolemma, "for their lives and in honor of their relatives the Bene Soade."[94] The location of the altar clearly indicates that here the title Lord of the World is intended for Baal Shamin, but we will see later that it should not be applied to him exclusively.

At the northern angle of the temple court the Swiss archaeologists uncovered an area which was used for the sacred repasts of the votaries of Baal Shamin.[95] This kind of religious precinct and the practice of offering sacred meals are well documented all over Syria. The meals in common were to strengthen the belief that the commensals formed a religious family devoted to, and in communion with, the deity in whose honor the repasts were celebrated.[96] These ceremonies were called at Palmyra and elsewhere *marzeah* (Greek *thiasos*), and the room in which the celebration took place was called *smk'*, a term equivalent to the Greek *kline*. One of the ashlars which served to form the couch in the dining room bears an inscription which reads: "In the month Elul, in the year 378 (September, 67) the votaries

[94] Dunant, *Les inscriptions*, p. 39, no. 25B.

[95] Collart and Vicari, *Architecture*, I, pp. 63–65.

[96] See F. E. Brown in *Dura-Europos: Preliminary Report* (cited in note 25 above), pp. 156–157; J. Teixidor, "Aramaic Inscriptions of Hatra," *Sumer* 20 (1964), 76–81, and B. Aggoula, "Une décanie à Hatra," *Semitica* 22 (1972), 53–55. It is worth noticing that in Mesopotamia there is "no trace" of this kind of *communio* between the deity and the faithful; see A. L. Oppenheim, *Ancient Mesopotamia: Portrait of a Dead Civilization* (Chicago: University of Chicago Press, 1964), p. 191.

of the *marzeaḥ* have made and offered this room to Baal Shamin and Duraḥlun, the good gods." On the contiguous ashlar another text gives the names of eighteen persons, all male, who either contributed toward the building or had become members of the group. Differences in the handwriting seem to indicate that the list of members was updated from time to time.[97]

Inscriptions concerning sacred banquets in honor of Palmyrene deities are innumerable. Most of the personnel devoted to the preparation and performance of these ceremonies appear time and again in the texts: butchers, cooks, bakers, cupbearers, musicians, smiths, etc. The tickets, or tesserae, used for the banquets were made of clay. Hundreds of them have been found, and they constitute a source of information of the first order. The tesserae bear all kinds of motifs and terms: representations of the deities to whom the banquets were dedicated, the names of the patron families, the functions performed by certain groups belonging to the main tribes of the city, the dates of the important festivities, the menus for certain banquets, cups, ladles, kraters, ovens, etc. The tesserae most probably were either sold or given by the votaries to friends and relatives.[98]

Some of the vessels used in these banquets have been recovered. Amphorae, each with a pointed bottom partially sunk in the floor of the dining area, are a common feature of the buildings dedicated to sacred banquets in the ancient Near East. The consumption of wine during the meals is well documented in the tesserae, and it is not difficult to find parallels to this practice among Nabataeans, Jews, Phoenicians, and, later on, Christians. The sacred banquets were eucharistic liturgies of a sort, and the Palmyrenes very

[97] Dunant, *Les inscriptions*, pp. 33–36.

[98] Milik, *Dédicaces*, pp. 141, 217, has studied in detail several aspects of the religious banquets. For the tesserae two books are essential: Ingholt et al., *Recueil des tessères de Palmyre* (cited in note 60 above), and R. du Mesnil du Buisson, *Les tessères et les monnaies de Palmyre* (Paris: E. de Boccard, 1962).

likely thought them to be the means by which to enter into communion with the divine. Contrary to the Christian eucharist in which there is a liturgical setting forth of the death of Christ (1 Cor. 10:16), the Palmyrene celebrations do not seem to have had a sacrificial character. Sacrifices, or "holocausts,"[99] were offered to the gods on the altars and never became related to the ceremonies of religious meals.

BEL AND BAAL SHAMIN

A stele found in the Camp of Diocletian some thirty years before Polish archaeologists excavated the area bears an inscription with a reference to a holocaust to be made to Baal Shamin. The text, in Greek, is written at the top of an aedicule in bas-relief in which a cluster of winged thunderbolts is represented. This is the symbol of Baal Shamin, the weather god. The inscription is incomplete, but the few sentences that can be reconstructed suggest that the date is 163 of our era and that the sacrifice is to be performed "every year, on the good day, for ever."[100] The "good day" is the sixth of Nisan, namely, the day on which the feast of Bel, Yarhibol, and Aglibol was celebrated at Palmyra. This celebration may be related to the beginning of the New Year, which in Babylonia took place in spring. The fact that the sixth of Nisan had a special meaning for the devotees of both Bel and Baal Shamin prompts the conclusion that the faithful did not look on the two gods as separate and independent deities.[101] In fact, Bel and Baal Shamin are systematically invoked in their inscriptions as *Zeus*,[102] and Zeus could be but one. The celebration of the

99 Milik, *Dédicaces*, pp. 3, 146–147.

100 H. Seyrig, *Syria* 14 (1933), 277–278. Milik, *Dédicaces*, pp. 145–146.

101 See Gawlikowski's remarks in *Le temple palmyrénien*, pp. 96–97, 110–111, regarding the inscription on the stele.

102 Bel: *CISem.*, II, 3942, 3970; *Inventaire*, III, ed. Cantineau (cited in note 62 above), no. 7; *Inventaire*, IX (cited in note 19 above), no. 26; Starcky, *Palmyre*, p. 88. Baal Shamin: Dunant, *Les inscriptions*, pp. 38–39, no. 25; ibid., pp. 55–56, no. 44.

sixth of Nisan that occurred simultaneously at the two main temples of the city acquires even greater relevance if it is remembered that Bel's cult was of Mesopotamian origin whereas that of Baal Shamin came to Palmyra from the Syro-Phoenician coast.

Baal Shamin was believed to be the Lord of the World. This title accords with and extends the conviction that he was the Lord to whom the heavens belonged. By making the thunderbolt his emblem the faithful acknowledged that Baal Shamin fully patronized the course of rains, winds, and crops. On the other hand, the supremacy of Bel was equally proclaimed by the Palmyrenes, although in a more elaborate manner. Bel was like the Babylonian Bel Marduk, peerless by right of conquest, and thus Bel is depicted on a frieze of the peristyle of his temple defeating a monster.[103] The scene evokes the victory of Bel Marduk over Tiamat, the monstrous personification of the primeval ocean, as described in the fourth tablet of the *Enuma elish*, the Creation story. In the Palmyrene relief the artist has represented Bel riding his chariot while, near the monster, a rider on horseback takes active part in the contest. Six other deities witness Bel's feat, impassive and bearing their characteristic attributes. From left to right they seem to be Šadrafa clutching the spear with an entwined snake, a goddess with a fish, her companion, a warrior god who most probably is Arṣu holding a round shield, Heracles leaning on his club, and a goddess of whom only the lower part of her robe is now visible.

It is unfortunate that the lack of archaeological and epigraphical evidence does not permit greater elaboration on the cults of Bel and Baal Shamin at Palmyra. It is tempting to stress, for instance, the importance that ritual processions might have had for the unification of the two cults. In the present state of Palmyrene studies, however, it is not easy to determine to what extent Babylonian culture

[103] Starcky, *Palmyre*, p. 88, pl. viii, 2, and Schlumberger, *L'Orient hellénisé* (cited in note 13 above), p. 89.

influenced Palmyra. M. Gawlikowski has argued that ritual processions must have taken place on the occasion of the New Year, following the tradition of the *Akitu* festival in Babylonia.[104] The feast of the New Year was celebrated there in the first eleven days of Nisan, the month which included the spring equinox. The climax of the celebration came when the statue of Marduk was borne from his sanctuary accompanied by the king. In the midst of communal jubilation the god passed along the Sacred Way, well paved and provided with splendid decorations,[105] on his way to a sanctuary outside Babylon. The ritual is well documented in Babylonian literature, but this is not the case at Palmyra, where no texts give the slightest hint of the New Year celebrations. To postulate the existence of processions in ancient Palmyra is a reasonable guess, but whether the displaying of Bel could have had any bearing on the unification of the cults of Bel and Baal Shamin into that of a supreme being who was Lord of the World, or whether the presence of two main temples, namely, those of Bel and Baal Shamin, must be taken as a sign that the two independent forms of cult were the result of the coexistence of two independent ethnic groups, are questions that remain as yet unanswered.

The fact that Baal Shamin is specifically invoked as *mare 'alma*, "Lord of the World,"[106] does not mean that this title is exclusively his. As a matter of fact the title suits Bel even better. In two inscriptions of A.D. 162 written on altars found in 1947/1948 at the spring of Efca,[107] the title "Lord of the World" refers most probably to Bel and not to Baal Shamin. In one of these inscriptions the donor of the offering ac-

---

[104] Gawlikowski, *Le temple palmyrénien*, pp. 82–83, 111; for the *Akitu* festival, see a résumé in H.W.F. Saggs, *The Greatness That Was Babylon* (New York: Hawthorn Books, 1966), pp. 383–389.

[105] Oppenheim, *Ancient Mesopotamia*, p. 139.

[106] Cooke, *North-Semitic Inscriptions* (cited in note 16 above), p. 296, no. 134; Starcky, *Palmyre*, pp. 98–99.

[107] Gawlikowski, *Inscriptions palmyréniennes* (cited in note 23 above), nos. 125–126.

knowledges that Yarhibol "appointed" him superintendent of the spring; for this official the association of Yarhibol with Bel, "Lord of the World," at the spring of Efca could present no difficulty since both gods had been united in the liturgy of the temple of Bel at the other end of the city.

The cult of Bel at Palmyra was very likely a copy of that of Bel Marduk in Babylonia. A cult of Bel appears here and there all over Syria. For Apamea, for instance, we have the precious information of Dio Cassius;[108] for other sites Greek inscriptions provide us with valuable information.[109] As is the case at Palmyra, the name *Bel* may represent in all those sites a shift, under the influence of Bel Marduk's cult, from a pronunciation *Bal/Bol*, the name of the Canaanite god, into that of *Bel*.

In the second half of the second millennium B.C. Bel Marduk achieved a position of supremacy in the Babylonian pantheon. According to the creation epic known in Akkadian as *Enuma elish*,[110] Marduk volunteered to fight against Tiamat, whereupon the assembly of the gods was called, and preeminence was granted to Marduk over the gods. Tablet IV of the text begins as follows:

> They erected for him a princely throne.
> Facing his fathers, he sat down, presiding.[111]
> Thou art the most honored of the great gods,
> Thy decree is unrivaled, thy command is Anu.[112]
> Thou, Marduk, art the most honored of the
>   great gods,
> Thy decree is unrivaled, thy word is Anu.
> From this day unchangeable shall be thy
>   pronouncement.
> To raise or bring low—this shall be (in) thy hand.

---

[108] Dio Cassius, *Roman History*, 79. 8. 5.

[109] See H. Seyrig, *Syria* 48 (1971), 86, note 2.

[110] *ANET*, pp. 60–72; trans. E. A. Speiser.

[111] Speiser: lit. "for advising"; see *ANET*, p. 66, note 63.

[112] Speiser: i.e., it has the authority of the sky-god Anu; see *ANET*, p. 66, note 64.

Thy utterance shall be true, thy command shall
    be unimpeachable.
No one among the gods shall transgress thy bounds!
Adornment being wanted for the seats of the gods,
Let the place of their shrines ever be in thy place.[113]
O Marduk, thou art indeed our avenger.
We have granted thee kingship over the universe
    entire.[114]

The election of Marduk preceded the creation of the
world. The chosen god had first defeated Tiamat. Once
the monster was killed, Marduk "paused to view her dead
body, that he might divide the monster and do artful
works."[115] And artful works they were. The dead body is
the matter from which heavens and earth were created.
Tablets v and vi offer a true cosmogonical recital of Marduk's works in which, as is well known, Genesis 1 and 2
find a remote parallel. Marduk is a creator god. *Enuma
elish* calls him "Lord of the Lands"; this is the fiftieth and
last name of the god.[116] The closing lines of the myth stress
Marduk's power:

The utterance of his mouth no god shall change.
When he looks he does not turn away his neck;
When he is angry no god can withstand his wrath.
Vast is his mind, broad his sympathy. . . .[117]

Within this cultural context the rights of Bel of Palmyra
to the title "Lord of the World" seem to be undisputed.

Any Semitic god whose name could be rendered in Greek
by Zeus was a true Lord of the World. This title and the
frequently used epithets "good" (*ṭb'*), "compassionate"
(*rḥmn'*), "merciful" (*tyr'*), "bountiful" (*škr'*), to all of
which the paraphrastic *epekoos*, "the one who listens to

---

113 This verse fully applies to the temple of Bel at Palmyra, which
was called "the house of the gods"; see pp. 116–117.

114 The passage quoted is from *ANET*, p. 66.

115 *ANET*, p. 67.   116 *ANET*, p. 72, note 155.

117 *ANET*, p. 72.

prayers," corresponds in the Greek inscriptions of Palmyra, usually accompany a supreme god; thus Bel and Baal Shamin are fully entitled to them. But Yarhibol, as the ancestral Baal of the spring of Efca, was very likely believed to deserve those epithets as well, for they occasionally follow the mention of the "anonymous" god in the altars offered to him in the vicinity of the spring. To be sure, the use of these epithets, which mirror the presence of a genuine piety, is not consistent and therefore no conclusion about the identity of a deity can be based exclusively on their appearance in a votive inscription.

Epithets such as "good," "compassionate," "the one who listens to prayers," etc., clearly indicate the Oriental character of both the gods thus invoked and the people who adored them. Neither the Phoenicans nor the Nabataeans ever used these divine epithets so profusely as the Palmyrenes did. A modern student of the history of religion may see in this peculiar behavior of the Palmyrenes a sign of their reliance on the gods. This, however, cannot be the whole truth.

Palmyra stands out in the Greco-Roman Near East as a cultural phenomenon, the history of which was that of the successive ethnic groups that settled there. Palmyra was the result of a process that in a few centuries changed familial and tribal associations into an urban confederation. The city achieved her ethnic cohesion[118] because she became the center of an international caravan traffic, and her glory declined when the Sasanians took over the commercial routes between Mesopotamia and Asia in the middle of the third century.[119] Palmyrene religion could not be untouched by that economic splendor. Indeed, Palmyra's pantheon appears as another accomplishment of her well-to-do citizens. The creation of the triad of Bel is a good example of it.

[118] By the middle of the second century of our era Palmyrene inscriptions no longer included the name of the tribe after the name of the individual; see Collart and Vicari, *Architecture*, I, p. 241.

[119] Février (cited in note 15 above), pp. 71–73.

ADDENDUM

1. Students of Palmyra have pointed out the existence
in the pantheon of the city of another triad, consisting of
Baal Shamin, Aglibol, and Malakbel, on the basis of two
reliefs; the first relief, in the Museum of the Louvre, por-
trays Baal Shamin between a Moon god, recognizable by
the crescent on his shoulders, and another deity.[120] The
second relief, exhibited in the Museum of Palmyra, shows
the supreme god in the form of an imposing eagle with
outspread wings, flanked by two deities represented only
by busts; one of them bears a crescent on his shoulders.[121]
There is no epigraphical evidence, however, to support the
thesis that the reliefs portray the triad of Baal Shamin. On
the other hand, occasional altars dedicated to "the Compassionate One" and to Aglibol and Malakbel,[122] or to "the
one whose name is blessed for ever" and to "the Holy Brothers,"[123] do not necessarily imply the presence of a triad.[124]
Baal Shamin in his character of Lord of Heaven was often
thought of in the ancient Near East as being accompanied
by the Moon god and the Sun god. In a treaty concluded in
the fourteenth century B.C. between Shuppiluliuma, king
of the Hittites, and Mattiwaza of Mitanni, the Hurrian
Lord of Heaven is invoked together with the Moon and
the Sun.[125] A similar religious formula is found in the Aramaic inscription of king Zakir of Hamath about the eighth
century B.C.[126] and in the boundary inscription of Gözne,

[120] Dimensions: h. 51 cm, w. 69 cm. First published by H. Seyrig, in
Syria 26 (1949), pl. II; see also *Syria* 48 (1971), p. 95, and Collart and
Vicari, *Architecture*, II, pl. CV, 2.

[121] Dimensions: h. 84 cm, w. 264 cm. Collart and Vicari, *Architecture*, II, pl. CV, 1.

[122] *CISem.*, II, 3981.   [123] *CISem.*, II, 4001, 4002.

[124] Milik, *Dédicaces*, p. 97, rejects the triad Baal Shamin, Aglibol, and
Malakbel to accept instead that of Baal Shamin, Duraḥlun, and Raḥim.

[125] E. F. Weidner, *Politische Dokumente aus Kleinasien*, Boghazköi-
Studien, 8 (Leipzig: Hinrichs, 1923), pp. 32–33, line 54.

[126] *KAI* 202.

in Asia Minor, from the Persian epoch.[127] But these texts bring forward only the logical unfolding of the concept of Baal Shamin as Lord of Heaven, i.e., of the firmament to which the sun and the moon belong, and following the tradition preserved in the Priestly document of Genesis 1:14–19, "the two great lights" were put there to separate the day from the night. Sun and moon thus give a meaning to the heavenly vault. This, however, does not entail any theological speculation on Baal Shamin's personality. The god was always adored alone, and the occasional presence of two accompanying deities does not constitute a triad.

2. The present study of religious texts from Palmyra has not taken into account all the minor gods, goddesses, and genii mentioned by the inscriptions. To deal with them in a systematic manner would have been as frustrating a task as to outline coherently the various and stupendous deeds of angels and saints in the Christian church.

[127] *KAI* 259, and BES 1970, p. 374, no. 82.

FIVE

PAGAN RELIGIOSITY

THE religious beliefs expressed in hundreds of Semitic inscriptions from the Persian and Greco-Roman periods put
forward no theological dogma, nor do they help students
of the history of religion reconstruct the myths of the origins of the world that the Palmyrenes accepted. Also missing is a body of ethical principles. The inscriptions usually
are nothing but bare acts of faith in the divine providence,
and as such they constitute a genuine expression of the daily
life of the Semites with whom they originated. But the lack
of theological information is a distressing fact for the historian.

Since no corpus of legal documents or of literary works
has yet been recovered from ancient Palmyra, the question
whether popular religion and religious dogma ever became
united there has to remain unanswered. Moreover, the inscriptions that so often mention the names of Bel and Baal
Shamin or invoke the "anonymous" god stop short of con-
veying the idea that these votive acts represented merely
aspects of the worship offered to the sole supreme god. The
fact is that when the names of Bel or Baal Shamin, or the
appellations "whose name is blessed for ever," "the Merciful
One," "Lord of the World," are translated from Palmyrene
into Greek the term *Zeus* is consistently used. This would
seem reason enough to conclude that the Palmyrenes adored
a single supreme ruler of the world were it not that such a
rationalistic approach sounds altogether anachronistic. So
far the data gained from the inscriptions must remain as
they are without placing them in a preconceived frame.

The student of Hellenistic religions, however, cannot pass
without notice the absence of myths in Nabataean and Pal-

myrene inscriptions. Religious texts are so succinct that when several deities are mentioned in a votive inscription their names are brought together without a hint at the possible links connecting them with one another.[1] To be sure, statues of the deities or reliefs depicting their symbols accompany at times the mention of a divine name. Among the symbols the cypress or the palm tree indicating the "holy garden" of Aglibol and Malakbel can be detected; a flying eagle stands for Baal Shamin; a hand holding thunderbolts is the symbol of the weather god; the representation of a starry sky and the zodiac in Bel's niche acknowledges his function as "Master of Fate";[2] the ram and the sheep were animals of Malakbel, patron of cattle and vegetation. But, in general, nothing—or very little—can be said about the deeds of Nabataean and Palmyrene deities. They seem to have been the object of private prayers exclusively.

There is here a striking dissociation between myth and private prayer. Dionysus, for instance, may be present at Palmyra in many personal names, and his image may decorate the ceiling of a temple or a tomb,[3] yet his cult is not attested by votive inscriptions, and altars were not erected to him. The presence of the god in Phoenicia or in the Hauran was very likely the result of Seleucid influence: Dionysus is profusely represented on Tyrian and Sidonian coins,[4] and his popularity in the Hauran was so great that Suweida was named after him.[5] Dionysus' true name, however, was concealed under the names of the local Semitic

[1] See *Inventaire des inscriptions de Palmyre*, XII, ed. A. Bounni and J. Teixidor (Beirut, 1976), nos. 54 and 55.

[2] See H. Seyrig, "Bêl de Palmyre," *Syria* 48 (1971), 89. A Latin inscription from Apamea says, *Belus Fortunae rector*; Dessau, 4333.

[3] Seyrig, *Syria* 48 (1971), 106, and H. Ingholt, "Quelques fresques récemment découvertes à Palmyre," *Acta archaeologica* 3 (1932), 15–16, pl. IV.

[4] W. W. Baudissin, *Adonis und Esmun* (Leipzig: Hinrichs, 1911), pp. 231–241, and G. F. Hill, *A Catalogue of the Greek Coins in the British Museum: Phoenicia* (London, 1910).

[5] See Ch. Three, note 44.

gods, for he is not mentioned in the inscriptions.[6] Of course, Dionysus' assimilation, with his thyros or his cornucopia, to a local god does not necessarily mean that Nabataeans, Arabs, or Palmyrenes accepted the particular mythic world in which Dionysus was a protagonist.

A similar situation exists with respect to the representation of Ganymede snatched up by an eagle on the ceiling of one of the best-preserved Palmyrene tombs.[7] The figure, squeezed in a circle and deprived of any mythological context, loses its religious value. The three brothers who constructed this T-shaped hypogeum, and who exploited it from A.D. 160 as a profitable family enterprise by leasing space for entombment, ordered the decoration, which the artist executed according to a fixed set of ornamental motifs.[8] The same purpose is served by the Medusa heads that appear on the walls of palaces and temples in Parthia, Syria, and Arabia.[9] The Greek Heracles was identified at Palmyra with Nergal, the Mesopotamian ruler of the realm of the dead,[10] yet the artists failed to show the chthonic aspect of

[6] See D. Sourdel, *Les cultes du Hauran à l'époque romaine* (Paris: Paul Geuthner, 1952), p. 63, and Seyrig, *Syria* 48 (1971), 107–109. In my opinion the various representations of Dionysus on the Palmyrene tesserae cannot justify the conclusion, apparently drawn by Seyrig, that orgiastic ceremonies were celebrated at Palmyra.

[7] J.-B. Chabot, *Choix d'inscriptions de Palmyre* (Paris: Imprimerie Nationale, 1922), p. 101, pl. XVI, 4; new photographs are reproduced in C. H. Kraeling, *Annales archéologiques de Syrie* 11–12 (1961–1962), 16, pl. XIII.

[8] Chabot, p. 104. Another motif executed by the artist was the scene showing Achilles dressed in woman's garb at the court of king Lycomedes; see Chabot, p. 101, and Kraeling, *Annales*, p. 16. One wonders how many Palmyrenes could understand the episode!

[9] See several examples in N. Glueck, *Deities and Dolphins* (New York: Farrar, Straus and Giroux, 1965), p. 643.

[10] See H. Seyrig, "Heracles-Nergal," *Syria* 24 (1945), 62–80, especially p. 65, where the author describes tessera no. 11 (which corresponds to no. 227 in Ingholt et al., *Recueil des tessères de Palmyre* [Paris: Paul Geuthner, 1955]); the tessera shows Heracles' club on one side and the name *nrgl*, "Nergal," on the other side.

the god; they usually portray him either with the club and the lion's skin or with the cuirass, the kalathos, and the double ax.[11]

In general, myths seem to have lost their relevance among the Semites of the last centuries of the first millennium B.C. The case of Edessa, in the province of Osrhoene, can be mentioned by way of example.

PAGANISM AT EDESSA

The kingdom of Edessa was founded by the Parthians around 130 B.C. after the city (Urhai, its native name; later, "Antioch by the Callirhoe") and the region had been for some hundred and seventy-five years under strong Seleucid influence.[12] Many of the rulers of the new dynasty had Arabic names; their language was Syriac—like Nabataean and Palmyrene, a branch of Aramaic. Arab nomads and seminomads populated the area: they were the *Saracens* mentioned by Ammianus Marcellinus and the Ṭayyaye of the Syriac chronicles. The Syriac inscriptions of the first three centuries of our era mention the existence of an officer called *shalliṭa dᵉ ʿArab*, "the ruler of ʿArab."[13]

[11] Only the latter attributes may denote a chthonic deity, the more so if the animal accompanying Heracles-Nergal at Palmyra is a dog and not a lion, as Seyrig has said; see note 10 above. Milik has discussed the problem in *Dédicaces*, pp. 166–169. A relief of greenish marble found at Hatra shows Nergal in frontal position, with a small diadem and horns, dressed in a Persian tunic and holding a dog with a triple head, which calls to mind Cerberos; see H. Ingholt, *Parthian Sculptures from Hatra: Memoirs of the Connecticut Academy of Arts and Sciences* 12 (New Haven, 1954), 32–33, pl. VII, 2. A good reproduction of the relief appears in R. Ghirshman, *Parthes et Sassanides* (Paris: Gallimard, 1962), pl. 98.

[12] See J. B. Segal, *Edessa: 'The Blessed City'* (Oxford: Clarendon Press, 1970), pp. 1–18.

[13] See H.J.W. Drijvers, *Old-Syriac (Edessean) Inscriptions* (hereafter *Inscriptions*), Semitic Study Series, n.s. III (Leiden: E. J. Brill, 1972), nos. 5, 3; 7, 2; 9, 4–5; 10, 4–5; and 23, 2. For the Syriac inscriptions in general, see note 22.

Edessa lay on the route taken by the caravans on their way to India and China. Some thirty miles southeast of the city was Harran, which in the sixth century B.C., under Nabonidus, the last king of Babylon, had reached the peak of its religious renown as the center of the cult of the Moon god. Another neighboring town was Batnae, which Ammianus Marcellinus described in the following manner: "The town of Batne, founded in Anthemusia in early times by a band of Macedonians, is separated by a short space from the river Euphrates; it is filled with wealthy traders when, at the yearly festival, near the beginning of the month of September, a great crowd of every condition gathers for the fair, to traffic in the wares sent from India and China, and in other articles that are regularly brought there in great abundance by land and sea."[14]

The region of Edessa was also open to commercial and cultural influences from Palmyra, Jerusalem, and Adiabene. The Jewish community in Edessa remained in contact with the first Judeo-Christian groups in Jerusalem, a factor which contributed to the early and rapid diffusion of Christianity in Osrhoene.[15] Greek culture, on the other hand, seems to

[14] Ammianus Marcellinus 14. 3. 3; trans. J. C. Rolfe, Loeb Classical Library (Cambridge, Mass., 1963), I, p. 25. Silk, of course, was an important article of trade; see Segal, *Edessa*, p. 137.

[15] This is manifest in the Syriac *Doctrine of Addai*, which reports the frequent contacts of Edessa with Jerusalem. When Addai, represented by legend as one of the seventy-two Apostles, went to Edessa, "he dwelt at the house of Tobias, son of Tobias the Jew, who was of Palestine" (*hw d'ytwhy hw' mn plstyn'*); see *The Doctrine of Addai, the Apostle*, ed. G. Phillips (London, 1876), text p. *h*, lines 9–11; trans. pp. 5–6. Despite its legendary character, the *Doctrine* is of great importance for the study of early Christianity. The document, in its present form, was written at the beginning of the fifth century; the legends, however, may well go back to the third century, as proved by a passage in Eusebius *Ecclesiastical History* (1. 13). At the time Eusebius wrote the final edition of the book (325) Edessa had had an active Christian community for more than one hundred and twenty-five years. The Judeo-Christian character of the Syriac-speaking Church in Osrhoene is obvious in the *Acts of Thomas* (third century) and in the *Odes of*

have made a strong impact upon the higher classes of the city. The *Book of the Laws of Countries* very plainly reveals through the dialogue of Avida and Bardesanes that Edessean intellectuals were acquainted with the fashionable theories of pagan and Christian Gnostics alike.[16] The reliable *Chronicle of Edessa*, in reporting the damage caused by the flood of November, 201, mentions informatively the great palace of king Abgar, the beautiful buildings of the city, and the temple of the Christians. It is said that after that tragic event king Abgar built a new winter palace and that the nobles imitated the monarch by building new mansions for themselves in a residential quarter known as Beth Shaḥraye.[17] Nothing is left today of that splendor but a

Solomon (second and third centuries); see H.J.W. Drijvers, *Bardaiṣan of Edessa* (Assen: Van Gorcum, 1966), pp. 209–210, for a good summary of the questions regarding date and authorship of these two texts. The Jewish participation in the trade between Osrhoene, Adiabene, Spasinou Charax, on the Persian Gulf, and Jerusalem has been studied by J. Neusner, *A History of the Jews in Babylonia*, 1: *The Parthian Period* (Leiden: E. J. Brill, 1965), pp. 88–93. For the political history of Nisibis, Singara, and Adiabene, see J. Teixidor, "The Kingdom of Adiabene and Hatra," *Berytus* 17 (1967), 4–8.

16 For the last edition and translation of the Syriac text, see H.J.W. Drijvers, ed., *The Book of the Laws of Countries: Dialogue on Fate of Bardaiṣan of Edessa*, Semitic Texts with Translation, III (Assen: Van Gorcum, 1965). The same author has discussed in a very valuable monograph on Bardesanes (*Bardaiṣan of Edessa*) the personality of the philosopher, his conception of God, Man, and the World and his influence on the Syriac-speaking early Church. Of great importance for the history of Christianity in Osrhoene is the chapter on Ephrem Syrus's attacks against Bardesanes and his school (Drijvers, ibid., pp. 127–165); see also H.J.W. Drijvers, "Bardaiṣan of Edessa and the Hermetica," *Jaarbericht Ex Oriente Lux* 21 (1969–1970), 190–210, and A.J.M. Davids, "Zur Kosmogonie Bardaiṣans: Textkritische Bemerkungen," *Zeitschrift der Deutschen Morgenländischen Gesellschaft* 120 (1970), 32–42.

17 Text and Latin translation in I. Guidi, ed., *Chronica minora*, Corpus scriptorum christianorum orientalium, Scriptores syri, ser. III, vol. 4 (Paris, 1903), pp. 1–13. See also I. Ortiz de Urbina, *Patrologia syriaca*, 2nd ed. (Rome: Pontificium Institutum orientalium studiorum, 1965), p. 206.

few mosaics that depict wealthy pagan families, attired with sophistication and allure, gathered around the paterfamilias.[18] Not all the mosaics, however, exhibit family portraits. A mosaic dated 235, for example, represents a funerary tower surmounted by the phoenix, the legendary bird of Egypt.[19] Another mosaic, of 228, illustrates the Orpheus theme: "the musician is seated, a lyre in his hand; around him are a lion, a gazelle, and birds in attitudes of becoming docility."[20]

Greek was used on coins and for documents. Edessean families liked to send their children to be educated in Beirut, Antioch, and Alexandria. The baths, the hippodrome, the pastimes reflect an urban society accustomed to the luxuries of the West.[21]

This was no doubt the world of the few, slightly touched by Western fashions. The bulk of the population, nonetheless, remained attached to the ancestral gods of the region, as the Syriac inscriptions recovered from Edessa, Sumatar Harabesi, Serrin, and Birtha (Birecik) clearly indicate. These texts, dated in the first three centuries of our era, are primarily funerary, but some of them have a bearing on the pagan cults of the region.[22] Notwithstanding the

---

[18] Segal, *Edessa*, pp. 39–41, pls. 1–3.

[19] Ibid., pl. 43. The legend of the phoenix was used by both pagan and Christian but not always for identical reasons. In Origen's *Contra Celsum*, for instance, Celsus uses the bird's instinct as an example of piety in irrational animals (4. 98), whereas for Clement of Rome the phoenix is an admirable symbol of the future resurrection (1 Clement 25).

[20] Segal, *Edessa*, p. 52, pl. 44.   [21] Ibid., pp. 29–35.

[22] Prior to the epigraphical discoveries made by J. B. Segal in the region of Edessa (modern Urfa) little was known about the Syriac-speaking communities of northern Mesopotamia. The inscriptions Segal found were published in the *Bulletin of the School of Oriental and African Studies* during the years 1954, 1957, 1959, and 1967. In 1971 H.J.W. Drijvers discovered new inscriptions in Sumatar Harabesi, in the Tektek Mountains some hundred kilometers southeast of Urfa, where Segal's first surveys proved to be so productive. A list of the inscriptions known by 1965 was published by E. Jenni in *Theologische*

presence of Macedonian colonists and despite several centuries of commercial activity with the West and the Far
East, the traditional cults remained alive. The Arab tribes
that settled in Osrhoene must have merged rapidly with
the local population, for the inscriptions which they left
behind invoke Sin, the ancient Moon god of Harran. Some
texts from Sumatar Harabesi call upon Sin simply as "the
god"[23] or, even more interestingly, as "Lord of the gods."[24]
An inscription from Kirk Mağara, outside Edessa, reads as
follows: "I, 'yw, daughter of Barshuma, made for myself
this burial place. I ask of you who come after and who may
enter here, move not my bones from the sarcophagus. He
that shall move my bones—may he have no latter-end, and
may he be accursed to the Lord of the gods."[25]

An Aramaic inscription of the second half of the eighth
century B.C. from Zinjirli had already invoked Sin as "Lord
of Harran,"[26] and the cuneiform steles of the reign of
Nabonidus found at Harran styled Sin precisely as "Lord
of the gods" and "the king of the gods."[27] The persistence
of the cult in this region is attested by Ammianus Marcel-

Zeitschrift 21 (1965), 371–385. Most recently Drijvers has collected all
the Syriac inscriptions of the first three centuries and has issued them
together in a very useful publication, Old-Syriac (Edessean) Inscriptions
(cited in note 13 above). It contains sixty-seven texts, to which the
author has added two inscriptions from Dura-Europos (no. 63 and pp.
54–57) and four coins. Finally, there should be mentioned the publication of F. Vattioni, "Le iscrizioni siriache antiche," in Augustinianum
12 (173), 279–338, with references to the inscriptions of Palmyra and
Hatra and a good translation of the texts.

[23] Drijvers, Inscriptions, nos. 13, 3, and 16, 2.

[24] Ibid., nos. 18, 3; 23, 3; and 24, 8.

[25] Segal, Edessa, p. 59. In the transcription of the personal name I
depart from Segal's interpretation to follow the reading proposed by
Drijvers, Inscriptions, no. 35, and by Vattioni, p. 304.

[26] See KAI 218 and II, p. 237. Zinjirli is the ancient Sam'al mentioned
in the inscriptions; for the history of the site, see A. Dupont-Sommer,
Les Araméens (Paris: A. Maisonneuve, 1949), pp. 66–68.

[27] See C. J. Gadd, "The Harran Inscriptions of Nabonidus," Anatolian Studies 8 (1958), 35–92, especially pp. 47–51, 56–65.

linus, who reports that Julian stopped at Harran in 363 on his way to Persia: "Having delayed there several days for necessary preparations, and to offer sacrifices according to the native rites of the Moon, which is religiously venerated in that region, before the altar, with no witness present, Julian is said secretly to have handed his purple mantle to his relative Procopius. . . ."[28]

These testimonies concerning the pagan life of Osrhoene are more compelling than the remarks made by the Syriac *Doctrine of Addai* regarding the cults practiced at Edessa in the first century of our era.[29] According to this book, Addai, the Apostle of Christ, gave the people gathered to hear him a grotesque picture of their idolatric cults; the Apostle made a specific allusion to Nebo and Bel as being the "idols" (*ptkr'*) worshiped by his audience. As is to be expected from this kind of propagandist writing, the audience easily gave up their idolatry after hearing the Apostle. The *Doctrine* states that later on even "the chiefs of the priests . . . ran and threw down the altars upon which they sacrificed before Nebo and Bel their gods, except the great altar, which was in the midst of the city."[30]

It is curious to read that "the great altar" (*'lt' rbt'*), which early in the book is mentioned as having been a matter of concern to the Apostle, is left untouched. Whatever this pagan altar may have been, its preservation indicates that the reference to the cults of Nebo and Bel is an erudite remark by the editor of the *Doctrine*. In fact, Nebo and Bel appear here as two stereotyped Mesopotamian deities deprived of the power they had enjoyed in the Near East during the Persian period.[31]

[28] Ammianus Marcellinus 23. 3. 2; trans. Rolfe, II, p. 321.

[29] I follow the edition of G. Phillips, *The Doctrine of Addai, the Apostle* (cited in note 15). For the date of the Syriac text, see also note 15.

[30] Ibid., text p. *ld*, lines 2–7; trans. Phillips, p. 32.

[31] After a triumphal entry into Babylon (October 29, 539 B.C.) Cyrus presented himself to the "oppressed" Babylonians as the one "whose

Faded Mythology

The continuous use of mythological themes in the monuments at Palmyra and in the Osrhoene had little or nothing to do with private piety. This lack of mythological enthusiasm is, of course, in sharp contrast with the oversimplifications of the pagan world publicized—and published—by the early Christian writers.

In a book of remarkable interest Jean Seznec has shown how the appearance early in the third century B.C. of the romance *Sacred Scripture* by Euhemerus of Messene had a decisive influence upon Greco-Roman intellectuals until early medieval times.[32] Euhemerus, as is well known, tried to put forward the thesis that all the gods in times long past had been human beings. The success of the book among his contemporaries, especially when it was translated from Greek into Latin, ensured its popularity during the first Christian centuries: "First the apologists, then the Fathers, seized eagerly upon this weapon which paganism itself has offered them, and made use of it against its polytheistic source."[33]

---

rule Bel and Nebo love, whom they want as king to please their hearts" (*ANET*, p. 316); A. L. Oppenheim has made interesting remarks on Cyrus's speech in *Ancient Mesopotamia* (Chicago: University of Chicago Press, 1964), pp. 152–153. Bel and Nebo are invoked on a funerary stele from Daskyleion (F. M. Cross, *BASOR* no. 184 [Dec. 1966], 7–13) as well as on an ostracon from Elephantine (P. Grelot, *Documents araméens d'Égypte*, Littératures anciennes du Proche-Orient, 5 [Paris: Les Éditions du Cerf, 1972], p. 350). By the time the two gods were mentioned by the *Doctrine* their reality must have been elusive; later on Jacob of Serug, bishop of Batnae in 519, still mentions them as gods of Edessa in his homily against idols; see "Discours de Jacques de Saroug sur la chute des idoles," Syriac edition trans. into French and ed. P. Martin, *Zeitschrift der Deutschen Morgenländischen Gesellschaft* 29 (1875), 107–147, especially p. 110, line 52, and p. 131.

[32] J. Seznec, *The Survival of the Pagan Gods: The Mythological Tradition and Its Place in Renaissance Humanism and Art*, trans. B. F. Sessions from the French, Bollingen Series, XXXVIII (Princeton: Princeton University Press, 1972), pp. 11–12.

[33] Ibid., p. 12.

In pages filled with erudition Clement of Alexandria, in the *Exhortation to the Greeks*, attacked the idolatrous cults by saying that the gods were really men: "the lands they dwelt in, the arts they practised, the records of their lives, yes, and their very tombs, prove conclusively that they were men."[34] In another, incongruous, passage Clement accuses the pagans of giving the same name, namely, *Zeus* to many different gods.[35]

Hundreds of miles away from Alexandria, in a cultural context different from Clement's, a Syriac homily known as the *Oration of Meliton the Philosopher* dealt with the pagan cults and their followers in much the same manner.[36] The *Oration* was probably composed in Osrhoene at the beginning of the third century of our era. Its author wrote one of the best pages of euhemeristic doctrine:

"The people of Argos made images for Hercules, because he was one of their own citizens and was brave, and slew by his valour noisome beasts, and more especially because they were afraid of him, for he was violent, and carried

[34] Clement of Alexandria *Exhortation to the Greeks* ch. 2. 25P; trans. C. W. Butterworth, Loeb Classical Library (Cambridge, Mass., 1960), p. 59. See also Tertullian *De idolatria* 15.

[35] Clement, p. 57. I confess to being unimpressed by Clement's statement. In fact, the use of *Zeus* for gods whose cults existed far apart from one another can be compared with the Semitic use of the term *baal* for any local—and usually supreme—god. While *Baal* and *El* were two proper names indicating two particular gods during the second millennium and the first centuries of the first millennium B.C., later on the tendency was to make Baal and even El appellatives of deities. In the first decades of the first century B.C. at Palmyra the very name of Ishtar ('*štr*) became synonymous with "goddess"; see *Inventaire des inscriptions de Palmyre*, XI, ed. J. Teixidor (Beirut, 1965), pp. 52–53, and Milik, *Dédicaces*, pp. 172–173. Of course, the existence of various *Zeuses* and of different biographies, as Clement says, would tend to eliminate local characteristics, emphasizing instead the cult of a supreme deity. When the Christian of the *Octavius* of Minucius Felix (end of the second century) says: *Nec Deo nomen quaeras. Deus nomen est,* "Seek not a name for God; the name is God" (par. 18), the statement must have been understood by pagans and Christians alike.

[36] In *Spicilegium syriacum*, ed. W. Cureton (Leiden, 1855), text pp. 22–35, trans, pp. 41–51.

away the wives of many, for his lust was great, like that of Zuradi [?] the Persian, his friend. Again, the people of Acte [read *Attica*] worshipped Dionysius, a king, because he originally introduced the vine into their country. The Egyptians worshipped Joseph, a Hebrew, who was called Serapis, because he supplied them with sustenance in the years of famine. The Athenians worshipped Athene, the daughter of Zeus, king of the island of Crete, because she built the citadel Athens, and made Ericthipus [read *Erichthonius*] her son king there, whom she had by adultery with Hephaestus, a smith, the son of a wife of her father; and she always was making companionship with Hercules, because he was her brother on her father's side. For Zeus the king fell in love with Alcmene, the wife of Electryon, who was from Argos, and committed adultery with her, and she gave birth to Hercules. The people of Phoenicia worshipped Balthi, queen of Cyprus, because she fell in love with Tamuz, son of Cuthar, king of the Phoenicians, and left her own kingdom, and came and dwelt in Gebal [i.e., *Byblos*], a fortress of the Phoenicians, and at the same time she made all the Cyprians subject to the king Cuthar:[37] for before Tamuz she had been in love with Ares, and committed adultery with him, and Hephaestus her husband caught her, and was jealous over her, and came and slew Tamuz in Mount Lebanon, while he was hunting wild boars; and from that time Balthi remained in Gebal, and she died in the city Aphaca, where Tamuz was buried.[38] The Elamites worshipped Nuh

[37] Queen Balthi (*blty mlkt' dkwprws*) is the goddess *b'lt* of the Byblian inscriptions. It is interesting to find here a close association between Tammuz and Kôshar, the epic figure of the Canaanite pantheon; see W. F. Albright, *Yahweh and the Gods of Canaan* (New York: Doubleday, 1968), pp. 135–137 and 147–148. Finally, mention should be made of the way in which the Phoenician colonization of Cyprus is presented to the reader in the *Oration*. The Phoenician presence on the island is archaeologically documented at Kition around 800 B.C., even though this may not mean a true colonization; see J. Teixidor, *American Journal of Archaeology* 78 (1974), 190. By 750–725 B.C. the king of Sidon had installed a governor on the island; see *KAI* 31.

[38] The Syriac writer has in mind Adonis; the identification of Adonis

[read *Anaitis*], daughter of the king of Elam. When the enemy had taken her captive, her father made for her an image and a temple in Shushan, a palace which is in Elam. The Syrians worshipped Athi [i.e., *Atargatis*], a Hadibite [i.e., an *Adiabenian*], who sent the daughter of Belaṭ, a doctor, to cure Simi, daughter of Hadad, king of Syria; and after a time, when the leprosy attacked Hadad himself, Athi entreated Elishah, the Hebrew, and he came and cured him of his leprosy. The people of Mesopotamia also worshipped Kutbi, a Hebrew woman,[39] because she delivered Bakru, the patrician of Edessa, from his enemies."[40]

The sarcastic remarks of the Apologists were directed, as Cumont has noted, against illusory enemies. The kind of

with Tammuz was known to Christian writers since the time of Origen; see Baudissin, *Adonis und Esmun* (cited in note 4), pp. 95–97. Baudissin has also studied this passage of Pseudo-Meliton in connection with a similar text of Theodore bar Koni (*Liber scholiorum*, ed. A. Scher, Corpus scriptorum christianorum orientalium, Scriptores syri, ser. II, vol. 60 [Paris, 1912], pp. 74–76). Aphaca is the site of the famous spring of Adonis. Its sacred character has been strengthened by Phoenician, Byzantine, and Muslim traditions. There stood a temple which the Emperor Constantine ordered demolished and which was partially rebuilt by Julian; see Baudissin, p. 363, note 1. For the present ruins, see D. Krencker and W. Zschietzschmann, *Römische Tempel in Syrien* (Berlin: W. de Gruyter, 1938), pp. 56–64; add the remarks of R. Donceel, "Recherches et travaux archéologiques récents au Liban," *L'antiquité classique* 35 (1966), 232.

39 The cult of the North-Arabic deity Aktab-Kutbâ is attested in Nabataean and Arabic inscriptions; see J. Starcky, *Suppl. DB*, VII, cols. 993–994. The qualification of *Kutbi* as a *Hebrew* woman (*kwtby 'bryt'*, *Spicilegium syriacum*, p. 25, line 13) is to be accepted very cautiously because Theodore bar Koni, toward the end of the eighth century, repeats Pseudo-Meliton's ideas, but he makes *kwzby* an *Arab* woman (*kwzby 'rbyt'*); see *Liber scholiorum*, ed. A. Scher (cited in note 38 above), II, p. 287, line 22. In view of the information offered by the Nabataean and Arabic inscriptions the interpretation of Theodore seems to be the correct one.

40 *Spicilegium syriacum*, ed. Cureton, pp. 43–44.

idolatry denounced by Clement, Pseudo-Meliton, or the *Doctrine of Addai* was long since extinct, to be found only in scholars "imbued with book learning" and "better acquainted with the opinions of ancient authors than with the sentiment of their contemporaries."[41] The derogatory approach of the Apologists to non-Jewish and non-Christian religion has been inherited by Western civilization without further reflection. The heirloom was accepted so uncritically that "pagan," according to the *Oxford English Dictionary*, is "one of a nation or community which does not worship the true God." This is an obvious *petitio principii*, which amounts to saying that monotheism is an exclusive patrimony of the Judeo-Christian tradition, wherein the ancient Near Eastern religions become examples of untrue religion. Judeo-Christian religion in the West has always been an assertive tradition which has too easily labeled "untrue" any form of religion outside its own.

Theophorous Names among the Semites

Any attempt to evaluate religious practices in the ancient Near East has to take into account the particular significance that personal names occasionally had. For the Semites a personal name was an inner force that shaped a person's future. In this sense it can be said that a personal name was a fate to go by. In the book of Genesis, for instance, the ancient editors often explain the meaning of the name given to a newborn child. The name expressed the being of its bearer. In the book of Hosea, chapter 1, the names of the children of the prophet's union with Gomer are "Not-pitied" (*Lo-Ruhama*) and "Not-my-people" (*Lo-Ammi*), and a feat of moral strength was needed to have the two names changed into those of "She-has-obtained-pity" and "My-people." There it was a successful revolt against the bearers' own destinies.

[41] Cumont, *Oriental Religions in Roman Paganism* (reprint ed., New York: Dover Publications, 1956), p. 203.

Curiously enough, the first Christians do not seem to have been much concerned with the theological meaning of names. By the middle of the third century pagan names were still used quite freely by Eastern and Western Christians alike.[42] Two reasons can explain this behavior. First, the conservative character of any society with regard to names. Parents usually choose from a set of well-established names. Today it is surprising to think that a name such as *John* made the relatives of Zakarias and Elizabeth protest, saying: "None of your kindred is called by this name" (Luke 1:61). Second, for the first Christians their "worldly" name did not count. The Acts of the Martyrs show that the name they wanted to be known by was that of "Christian." Augustine himself in his *Confessions* (6. 4. 5) states that the name of Christ had been put upon him as a child.[43]

Nowadays names and surnames mean nothing, but they had a meaning in the past. Some English surnames, for instance, derive from terms for manual work, commerce, municipal life, household, court, church, and learning. Rank and status also are important in name-producing: freeman, master, bond, burgess, etc. Surnames derived from appearance and behavior are, of course, countless. And so are names derived from close familiarity: David becomes Daw, Richard Hick, and Roger Hodge (or Dodge, by the frequent habit of rhyming). Surnames derived from place names are plentiful, and they cover both the different features of the landscape in which the homestead may have been situated (brook, hill, lane, moore, dean) and the actual names of villages, towns, and counties.[44]

The various patterns from which most of our modern names and surnames have originated can be easily found in all the Semitic onomastics; Akkadian, Ugaritic, Phoenician,

[42] A. Harnack, *The Mission and Expansion of Christianity . . .* (New York: Harper and Row, Harper Torchbook, 1962), pp. 422–430.

[43] Ibid., p. 424.

[44] These remarks about English names have been collected from C. M. Matthews, *English Surnames* (New York: Charles Scribner's Sons, 1966).

Hebrew, Aramaic, Syriac, and Arabic names also are formed from occupational names, nicknames, and toponymies. The highest proportion, however, correspond to the so-called theophorous names, which represent a phenomenon analogous to the role played by the names of the saints in European onomastics.[45]

A theophorous name is usually given when a child is born; thus names reflect the parents' piety toward the god under whose protection the newborn is placed. A theophorous name conveys the anxieties, the joy, and the expectations of the parents.[46]

The names which are the easiest to understand are the soothsaying names: *nomen* is *omen*. Names showing confidence in the god as being "the shelter" (Arabic *'wd*) of the newborn: *Avidallat* ("Protégé of Allat") or *Avidashur*. *Audelos* is the Greek transcription of a name probably

---

[45] Ibid., pp. 233–243, where the author studies the names derived from such favorite saints as Nicholas, Martin, Maurice, Lawrence, and Benedict. Nicholas in all its forms is "easily ahead of the others," and she explains: "At all times the influence of women must have been great in naming children, and it is no wonder that mothers longing for special protection for their newborn sons should choose St. Nicholas, the patron Saint of children" (p. 233).

[46] A. Caquot has written an important study on this subject: "Sur l'onomastique religieuse de Palmyre," *Syria* 39 (1962), 231–256. My remarks follow his closely. Basic bibliography for my study is: M. Noth, *Die israelitischen Personennamen im Rahmen der gemeinsemitischen Namengebung*, Beiträge zur Wissenschaft vom Alten und Neuen Testament, III, vol. 10 (Stuttgart, 1928); H. B. Huffmon, *Amorite Personal Names in the Mari Texts* (Baltimore: Johns Hopkins University Press, 1965); F. Gröndahl, *Die Personennamen der Texte aus Ugarit* (Rome: Pontificium Institutum Biblicum, 1967); J. K. Stark, *Personal Names in Palmyrene Inscriptions* (Oxford: Clarendon Press, 1971); F. L. Benz, *Personal Names in the Phoenician and Punic Inscriptions* (Rome: Biblical Institute Press, 1972); K. L. Tallqvist, *Assyrian Personal Names*, Acta Societatis Scientiarum Fennicae, XLIII (Helsingfors, 1914); J. Cantineau, *Le Nabatéen*, II (Paris: E. Leroux, 1932), pp. 55–158; H. Wuthnow, *Die semitischen Menschennamen in griechischen Inschriften und Papyri des vorderen Orients* (Leipzig: Dieterich, 1930); for Syriac personal names, see F. Vattioni's article cited in note 22.

meaning "Protection of El," and *Audu* seems to be its hypocoristic form. To the same category belong the names which confess that the deity is "the wall" that will protect the newborn: *Belshur, Nebushur.* A similar pattern is found in Israelite names.[47] Deities are occasionally styled "the good luck" (*gad*) of the child (*Gaddibol, Gaddarsu*) or his "light" (*nwr*); the latter has produced theophorous names in all the Semitic ethnic groups (*Nurbel, Nurathe, Betelnuri*). Names with the element *'r, ur,* "light," are found in Hebrew, Ugaritic, Ammorite, and Phoenician onomastics.

Faith in divine action upon the child can also be acknowledged by means of verbal sentences, which in general indicate that the deity "shows favor" (*Hannibal*), "heals" (*Raphael*), "sees" (*Hazael*), "makes the route easy" (*b'lpls*), "knows" (*Yedibel,* i.e., "Known to Bel"), "saves" (*Eshmunḥileṣ*), "listens" (*Melqartshamaʿ*), or "gives" (*Sidiathon, Mattanbaal,* and *Mattebol,* "Gift of the Lord").

The last of these names belongs in the category of appellations that mirror the gratitude of the parents toward the deity. The Aramaean newborn who received the name of *Phaṣael* was certainly a much-wanted child, for his name means "God has opened [the womb]." This name has parallels in Hebrew and Phoenician.[48] Theophorous names with the element *brk,* "to bless": *Barekshamash, Barekbaal, Bolbarek,* ought to be considered as belonging to this category,[49] the idea being that the deity "has blessed" the parents with a son. The element *grm,* "to decide," is used in theophorous names; for instance, *Sampsigeram,* to indicate that the god "has decided" the birth of the child.[50] The name *Baalshapaṭ,* "The Lord has judged," can easily be a reference to the particular circumstances in which a child was born. Names with the element *ndb* are numerous: *Yehonadab* or *Nadibel,* for instance, mean that Yahweh or Bel has been generous

[47] See Caquot, *Syria* 39 (1962), 242–243, and Noth, p. 157.
[48] See Stark, p. 109; Noth, p. 179; and Benz, p. 396.
[49] Caquot, *Syria* 39 (1962), 246.   [50] Ibid., pp. 246–247.

toward the parents.[51] The parents may exclaim at the moment the child is born: "God is great!" or the like. These first exhilarated reactions of the parents are to be taken as the origin of many names: *Rabbel*, "Great is El"; *Elbaal*, "El is the Lord"; *Michael*, "Who is like El?"; *Abinadab*, "The god my Father is generous"; *Aḥiram*, "[The god] my Brother is exalted."

The compulsive force of the name is nowhere as obvious as in the overwhelming use of the term "servant" in Semitic onomastics. From the very first moment the child's name "Servant of [this or that deity]," sets the type of life which the newborn is asked to lead. This type of name echoes the ancient Mesopotamian belief—expressed in the first stories of the creation of the world—that man was created for the benefit of the gods: man was to serve the gods. This is the purpose which Marduk had in mind when he announced the creation of man to his father, the wise Ea:

> Blood I will mass and cause bones to be.
> I will establish a savage, "man" shall be his name.
> Verily, savage-man I will create.
> He shall be charged with the service of the gods
> That they might be at ease![52]

Theophorous names made with the element "servant" (*'bd, tym*) illustrate the particular cults favored by the parents: Bel, Shamash, Allat, Nebo, El, Melqart, Eshmun, etc. Each family had its own divine patron, their *gad*, namely, the "fortune" of the family or tribe. This worship is to be identified with that of "the god of the fathers."[53] Biblical

[51] Ibid., p. 245; for the Assyrian names, see Tallqvist, p. 296, and for the Hebrew ones Noth, p. 193. Josephus (*J. Ant.* 8. 35–36) mentions names such as *Abinadabos, Achinadabos*, etc.; see Benz, p. 359.

[52] *Enuma elish*, tablet VII, 5–8: *ANET*, p. 68.

[53] See A. Alt, *Der Gott der Vater* published in 1929 and republished in A. Alt, *Kleine Schriften zur Geschichte des Volkes Israel*, I (Munich: Beck, 1953), pp. 1–78. There is an English translation of the article in *Old Testament History and Religion*, trans. R. A. Wilson (New York: Doubleday, Anchor Books, 1966), pp. 3–98. The reservations of

texts as well as Phoenician and Aramaic inscriptions from the beginning of the first millennium B.C. on provide ample evidence for the existence of such a cult. Royal inscriptions, Phoenician and Aramaic alike, invoke either the god of the dynasty or the god of the king, and later inscriptions from the Hauran or from Palmyra also mention the god of the family or the individual.[54]

Semitic religion is no doubt individualistic, but at the same time the acceptance by successive members of a family of the cult of the same deity made the latter become "ancestral." The importance of the "ancestral" gods among the Semites of Syro-Phoenicia and North Arabia is seldom emphasized by students of the history of religion, yet its relevance is such that by itself it may help settle the discussion about Semitic monotheism.

Monotheism implies the categorical denial of the existence of other gods. This denial may grow out from prophetic insight or from philosophical reflection. The author of Second Isaiah (chapters 40–55) admits that there is no god beside Yahweh, and centuries of formal theological reflection in the tradition of the Greek philosophers have made monotheism become the outcome of the doctrine of God as the first cause of the world. None of the inscriptions presented here in any way proclaimed the exclusive prerogatives of one god; consequently, none can strictly speaking be termed monotheistic. Yet a trend toward a practical monotheism is there manifest. The authors of the inscriptions

F. M. Cross regarding Alt's article (*Canaanite Myth and Hebrew Epic* [Cambridge, Mass.: Harvard University Press, 1973], pp. 3–12) do not affect my own interpretation cf the extrabiblical material.

[54] For the royal inscriptions, see Kilamuwa, *KAI* 24, lines 15–16 (ca. 825 B.C.); Yehawmilk, *KAI* 10, 2 (fifth century B.C.); *zkr*, king of Hamath, *KAI* 202A (eighth century B.C.); Panamu, *KAI* 215, 22 (second half of the eighth century B.C.); Barrakib, *KAI* 217, 3. For the later inscriptions, see Sourdel, *Les cultes du Hauran* (cited in note 6 above), pp. 95–97; C. C. McCown, "The Goddesses of Gerasa," *Annual of the American School of Oriental Research* 13 (1931–1932), 145–149; Milik, *Dédicaces*, pp. 73–74.

worshiped a supreme god who was alone in possessing a power that excelled any other divine power. He was believed to be a Weather god; heaven belonged to him. Lesser gods were his messengers and ministers. As stated in the first chapter, the cult of the angels became a significant feature of the religious life of the Near East during the Persian and Hellenistic times. It gave the angels their role of messengers but also stressed the fact that the Lord of Heaven ranked at the top of a hierarchy of divine beings. On the other hand, the religious life of the various groups whose inscriptions have been studied in the preceding pages was rooted in the tradition of the ancestors. The faith of a family, a tribe, or a dynasty in its ancestral gods made the latter be unique and trustworthy. Unique because the family, the tribe, or the dynasty was brought up to believe that it was different from other families, tribes or dynasties, and so were its gods; trustworthy because the ancestral gods had to listen to the prayers of those who were their people. In this context the existence of other peoples' gods ought not to be a matter of concern: they could be easily ignored. Discussion of the existence among the ancient Semites of a monotheistic cult should, it would seem, become pointless whenever the ancestral cult of a supreme god is acknowledged.[55]

[55] The question of the god of the fathers in the ancient Near East seems to me to be more a matter for philosophical consideration than an issue to be dealt with by the Semiticist whose world is often narrowed by philological queries. Epigraphy is only an auxiliary to history, in our case, to history of religion. By interpreting the ancient texts in the light of his Western culture the Semiticist risks forgetting altogether that the very cult of the ancestral gods was one of the parochial pursuits that shaped the idiosyncrasy of the group or tribe. Recent studies on linguistics show that "all developed language has a private core," and that words "encode, preserve, and transmit the knowledge, the shared memories, the metaphorical and pragmatic conjectures on life of a small group—a family, a clan, a tribe" (G. Steiner, *After Babel: Aspects of Language and Translation* [New York: Oxford University Press paperback, 1976], p. 231). If, as Steiner says, in the beginning the word was a password "granting admission to a nucleus of like speakers" (p. 231), the ancestral religious beliefs of any group could not have

Phoenicians, Aramaeans, or Arabs did not need "proof"
to believe in their own gods: the gods had been worshiped
by their families for generations, therefore when the fool
of Psalm 14 says: "There is no god" he is not turning down
a philosophical postulate, he is simply revolting against tradition to proclaim that he wants to live as if there were no
god to be served.

St. Anselm (1033–1109), as is well known, rebutted the
fool's statement in the so-called ontological argument. According to Anselm, the mere definition of God leads logically
to the assertion of his existence. It is important to bear in
mind that the argument in the *Proslogium* forms part of an
address to God. The philosopher refuted the fool while im-
mersed in his spiritual meditation.[56] As a reaction to the
outburst of the fool and within the context of the psalm
Anselm's speculation produces embarrassment. The fool in
his "existentialist" statement and Anselm in the rationalization of his faith in God's existence are worlds apart, worlds
that cannot be reconciled.

---

been less esoteric. The religious drive of an ancient tribe was inward
and, therefore, its concept of god—the god of its ancestors—was likely to
generate convictions as powerful as those cherished by the followers of
Judaism, Christianity, or Islam.

[56] Briefly the argument runs as follows: God is that being than which
no greater one can be imagined, and the fool thinks that such a being
exists only in the imagination, not in reality. But if that being of
which no greater one can be imagined exists in reality, he would be
God, for he would have something which the being imagined by the
fool does not have, namely, existence.

ARCHAEOLOGICAL AND LITERARY SOURCES

1. SEMITIC INSCRIPTIONS. COLLECTIONS OF TEXTS IN VARIOUS LANGUAGES.

[*ANET*] *Ancient Near Eastern Texts Relating to the Old Testament*, ed. James B. Pritchard, 2nd ed. (Princeton: Princeton University Press, 1955).

The Ancient Near East: Supplementary Texts and Pictures Relating to the Old Testament, ed. James B. Pritchard (Princeton: Princeton University Press, 1969).

Cooke, G. A., *A Text-Book of North-Semitic Inscriptions* (Oxford: Clarendon Press, 1903).

[*CISem.*] *Corpus inscriptionum semiticarum, pars prima* [Phoenician inscriptions]; *pars secunda* [Aramaic inscriptions] (Paris: C. Klincksieck, 1881–).

[*KAI*] Donner, H., and W. Röllig, *Kanaanäische und aramäische Inschriften*, I (2nd ed., Wiesbaden: Otto Harrassowitz, 1966); II (2nd ed., ibid., 1968); III (1964).

Dussaud, R., and F. Macler, *Voyage archéologique au Ṣafâ et dans le Djebel ed-Drûz* (Paris: E. Leroux, 1901).

Lidzbarski, M., *Ephemeris für semitische Epigraphik*, 3 vols. (Giessen: A. Töpelmann, 1900–1915).

[BES] Teixidor, J., "Bulletin d'épigraphie sémitique," in *Syria* from 1967 on.

Winnett, F. V., and W. L. Reed, *Ancient Records from North Arabia* (Toronto: University of Toronto Press, 1970).

Akkadian

Dossin, G., "Quelques textes inédits de Mari," *Comptes rendus de la première rencontre assyriologique internationale, Paris, 26–28 juin 1950* (Leiden: E. J. Brill, 1951), 19–21.

———, *Correspondance de Iasmaḫ-Addu*, Archives royales de Mari, ed. A. Parrot and G. Dossin, V (Paris: Imprimerie Nationale, 1952).

Eisser, G., and J. Lewy, *Die altassyrischen Rechtsurkunden vom Kültepe*, 3–4, *Mitteilungen der Vorderasiatisch-Ägyptischen Gesellschaft* 35, pt. 3 (Leipzig, 1935).

Gadd, C. J., "The Harran Inscriptions of Nabonidus," *Anatolian Studies* 8 (1958), 35–92.

Knudtzon, J. A., ed., *Die El-Amarna-Tafeln*, Vorderasiatische Bibliothek, 2 (Leipzig: Hinrichs, 1915).

Nougayrol, J., *Le Palais royal d'Ugarit*, iv: *Textes accadiens des Archives Sud (Archives internationales)*, Mission de Ras Shamra, ix (Paris: Imprimerie Nationale, 1956).

Weippert, M., "Die Kämpfe des assyrischen Königs Assurbanipal gegen die Araber: Redaktionskritische Untersuchung des Berichts in Prisma A," *Die Welt des Orients* 7 (1972), 38–85.

Aramaic

Cowley, A., *Aramaic Papyri of the Fifth Century B.C.* (Oxford: Clarendon Press, 1923).

[*BASOR*] Cross, F. M., "An Aramaic Inscription from Daskyleion," *Bulletin of the American Schools of Oriental Research*, no. 184 (Dec. 1966), 7–10.

Grelot, P., *Documents araméens d'Égypte*, Littératures anciennes du Proche-Orient, 5 (Paris: Les Éditions du Cerf, 1972).

Kraeling, E. G., *The Brooklyn Museum Aramaic Papyri* (New Haven: Yale University Press, 1953).

Milik, J. T., "Les papyrus araméens d'Hermoupolis et les cultes syro-phéniciens en Égypte perse," *Biblica* 48 (1967), 546–621.

Rabinowitz, I., "Aramaic Inscriptions of the Fifth Century B.C.E. from a North-Arab Shrine in Egypt," *Journal of Near Eastern Studies* 15 (1956), 1–9.

Starcky, J., "Une tablette araméenne de l'an 34 de Nabuchodonosor," *Syria* 37 (1960), 99–115.

Hatrean

Aggoula, B., "Remarques sur les inscriptions hatréennes," *Berytus* 18 (1969), 85–104.

———, "Remarques sur les inscriptions hatréennes, II," *Mélanges de l'Université Saint-Joseph* 47 (1972), 3–80.

———, "Une décanie à Hatra," *Semitica* 22 (1972), 53–55.

Caquot, A., "Nouvelles inscriptions araméennes de Hatra," *Syria* 19 (1952), 89–118; 30 (1953), 234–246; 32 (1955), 49–58; 261–272; 40 (1963), 1–16; 41 (1964), 251–272.

Degen, R., "Neue aramäische Inschriften aus Hatra," *Die Welt des Orients* 5 (1970), 222–236.

Ingholt, H., "Inscriptions from Hatra," in *An Aramaic Handbook*, ed. F. Rosenthal, I, pt. 1 (Wiesbaden: Otto Harrassowitz, 1967), pp. 44–50.

Teixidor, J., "Aramaic Inscriptions of Hatra," *Sumer* 20 (1964), 77–80.

———, "The Altars Found at Hatra," *Sumer* 21 (1965), 85–92.

Nabataean

Cantineau, J., *Le Nabatéen*, II: *Choix de textes; lexique* (Paris: E. Leroux, 1932).

Jaussen, A. J., and R. Savignac, *Mission archéologique en Arabie*, I (Paris: E. Leroux, 1909); II (Paris: Paul Geuthner, 1914).

Littmann, E., *Semitic Inscriptions*, sect. A: *Nabataean Inscriptions*, Publications of the Princeton University Archaeological Expeditions to Syria in 1904–1905 and 1909, div. IV (Leiden: E. J. Brill, 1914).

Milik, J. T., "Nouvelles inscriptions nabatéennes," *Syria* 35 (1958), 227–251.

———, "Inscriptions grecques et nabatéennes de Rawwafah," in Parr et al., "Preliminary Survey . . . , 1968," under no. 6 below.

Negev, A., "Nabataean Inscriptions from 'Avdat (Oboda)," *Israel Exploration Journal* 13 (1963), 113–124.

[*Supp. DB*] Starcky, J., "Pétra et la Nabatène," in *Supplément au Dictionnaire de la Bible*, VII (Paris: Letouzey & Ané, 1964), cols. 886–1017.

Palmyrene

Cantineau, J., "Tadmorea," *Syria* 14 (1933), 169–202 (nos. 1–16); 17 (1936), 267–282 (nos. 17–20) and 346–355 (nos. 21–27); 19 (1938), 72–82 (nos. 28–35) and 153–171 (nos. 36–46).

Chabot, J.-B., *Choix des inscriptions de Palmyre* (Paris: Imprimerie Nationale, 1922).

Dunant, C., *Le sanctuaire de Baalshamin à Palmyre*, III: *Les inscriptions*, Bibliotheca helvetica romana, X (Neuchâtel: P. Attinger, 1971).

Gawlikowski, M., *Le temple palmyrénien*, Palmyre, VI (Warsaw, 1973).

———, *Recueil d'inscriptions palmyréniennes provenant de fouilles syriennes et polonaises récentes à Palmyre* (Paris: Imprimerie Nationale-C. Klincksieck, 1974).

Al-Hassani, Dj., and J. Starcky, "Autels palmyréniens découverts près de la source Efca," *Annales archéologiques de Syrie* 3 (1953), 145–164; 7 (1957), 95–122. (The inscriptions have been republished in Gawlikowski, *Recueil d'inscriptions palmyréniennes*. . . .)

Ingholt, H., H. Seyrig, J. Starcky, and A. Caquot, *Recueil des tessères de Palmyre*, Bibliothèque archéologique et historique, LVIII (Paris: Paul Geuthner, 1955).

Inventaire des inscriptions de Palmyre, I–IX, ed. J. Cantineau (Damascus, 1930–1936); X, ed. J. Starcky (Damascus, 1949); XI, ed. J. Teixidor (Beirut, 1965); and XII, ed. A. Bounni and J. Teixidor (Beirut, 1976).

Mesnil du Buisson, R. du, *Inventaire des inscriptions palmyréniennes de Doura-Europos* (Paris: Paul Geuthner, 1939).

———, *Tessères et monnaies de Palmyre: Planches* (Paris: Bibliothèque Nationale, 1944).

———, *Les tessères et les monnaies de Palmyre* (Paris: E. de Boccard, 1962).

[*Dédicaces*] Milik, J. T., *Recherches d'épigraphie proche-orientale*, I: *Dédicaces faites par des dieux (Palmyre, Hatra, Tyr) et des thiases sémitiques à l'époque romaine*, Bibliothèque archéologique et historique, XCII (Paris: Paul Geuthner, 1972).

Schlumberger, D., *La Palmyrène du Nord-Ouest* [inscriptions edited by H. Ingholt and J. Starcky], Bibliothèque archéologique et historique, XLIX (Paris: Paul Geuthner, 1951).

Starcky, J., "Inscriptions archaïques de Palmyre," *Studi orientalistici in onore di Giorgio Levi Della Vida*, II (Rome: Istituto per l'Oriente, 1956), pp. 509–528.

———, "Relief dédié au dieu Mun'îm," *Semitica* 22 (1972), 57–65.

Phoenician and Punic

Berthier, A., and R. Charlier, *Le sanctuaire punique d'El-Hofra à Constantine* (Paris: Arts et métiers graphiques, 1955).

[*BASOR*] Cross, F. M., and R. J. Saley, "Phoenician Incantations on a Plaque of the Seventh Century B.C. from Arslan Tash in Upper Syria," *Bulletin of the American Schools of Oriental Research*, no. 197 (Feb. 1970), 42–49.

Dunand, M., and R. Duru, *Oumm el-'Amed*, Librairie d'Amérique et d'Orient (Paris: A. Maisonneuve, 1962).

Dupont-Sommer, A., "Une inscription phénicienne archaïque récemment trouvée à Kition (Chypre)," *Mémoires de l'Académie des Inscriptions et Belles-Lettres* 44 (1970), 9–28.

Fantar, M., "Les inscriptions," in E. Acquaro et al., *Ricerche puniche ad Antas*, Studi semitici, 30 (Rome: Istituto di studi del Vicino Oriente, 1969), pp. 47–93.

Guzzo Amadasi, M. G., *Le iscrizioni fenicie e puniche delle colonie in occidente*, Studi semitici, 28 (Rome: Istituto di studi del Vicino Oriente, 1969), pp. 47–93.

———, "Un'iscrizione fenicia da Cipro," *Rivista di studi fenici* 1 (1973), 129–134.

Masson, O., and M. Sznycer, *Recherches sur les Phéniciens à Chypre*, Centre de recherches d'histoire et de philologie, École pratique des Hautes Études, ser. II, no. 3 (Paris and Geneva: Droz, 1972).

Peckham, J. B., *The Development of the Late Phoenician Scripts*, Harvard Semitic Series, XX (Cambridge, Mass.: Harvard University Press, 1968).

Weippert, M., "Elemente phönikischer und kilikischer Religion in den Inschriften vom Karatepe," *Zeitschrift der Deutschen Morgenländischen Gesellschaft*, suppl. 1: *XVII. Deutscher Orientalistentag, 1968* (Wiesbaden: Franz Steiner, 1969), pp. 191–217.

Syriac

Drijvers, H.J.W., *Old-Syriac (Edessean) Inscriptions*, Semitic Study Series, n.s. III (Leiden: E. J. Brill, 1972).

Jenni, E., "Die altsyrischen Inschriften 1.–3. Jahrhundert n. Chr.," *Theologische Zeitschrift* 21 (1965), 371–385.

Segal, J. B., *Edessa, 'The Blessed City'* (Oxford: Clarendon Press, 1970).

Vattioni, F., "Le iscrizioni siriache antiche," *Augustinianum* 13 (1973), 279–338.

2. GREEK AND LATIN INSCRIPTIONS

Avi-Yonah, M., "Mount Carmel and the God of Baalbek," *Israel Exploration Journal* 2 (1952), 118–124.

———, "Syrian Gods at Ptolemais-Accho," *Israel Exploration Journal* 9 (1959), 1–12.

Bruneau, P., *Recherches sur les cultes de Délos à l'époque hel-*

lénistique et à l'époque imperiale, Bibliothèque des Écoles françaises d'Athènes et de Rome, fasc. 217 (Paris: E. de Boccard, 1970).

Dessau, H., ed., *Inscriptiones latinae selectae,* 3 vols. (Berlin: Weidman, 1892–1916).

Dittenberger, W., *Sylloge inscriptionum graecarum,* 3rd ed., F. H. von Gaertringen, 4 vols. (Leipzig: S. Hirzel, 1915–1924).

Milik, J. T., *Dédicaces,* see under no. 1, Semitic inscriptions: Palmyrene.

Milne, J. G., *Greek Inscriptions,* Service des antiquités de l'Égypte, Catalogue général des antiquités égyptiennes du Musée du Caire (Oxford: Oxford University Press, 1905).

Prentice, W. K., *Greek and Latin Inscriptions: Northern Syria,* Publications of the Princeton University Archaeological Expeditions to Syria in 1904–1905 and 1909, div. III, sect. B (Leiden: E. J. Brill, 1922).

Rey-Coquais, J.-P., *Inscriptions grecques et latines de la Syrie,* VI: *Baalbek et Beqa',* Bibliothèque archéologique et historique, LXXVIII (Paris: Paul Geuthner, 1969).

———, ibid., VII: *Arados et régions voisines,* ibid., LXXIX (ibid., 1970).

Roussel, P., and M. Launey, *Inscriptions de Délos,* Académie des Inscriptions et Belles-Lettres, IV (Paris, 1937).

Seyrig, H., "Nouveaux monuments palmyréniens des cultes de Bêl et de Baalshamîn," *Syria* 14 (1933), 253–282.

———, "Le statut de Palmyre," *Syria* 22 (1941), 155–174.

———, "Inscriptions grecques de l'agora de Palmyre," *Syria* 22 (1941), 223–270.

Waddington, W. H., *Inscriptions grecques et latines de la Syrie* (Paris, 1870).

Welles, C. B., *Royal Correspondence in the Hellenistic Period: A Study in Greek Epigraphy* (New Haven: Yale University Press, 1937).

———, R. O. Fink, and J. F. Gilliam, eds., *The Excavations at Dura-Europos, Final Report,* V, pt. 1: *The Parchments and Papyri* (New Haven: Yale University Press, 1959).

3. Greek and Latin Authors

The following passages have been quoted:
Ammianus Marcellinus *Res gestae* 14. 3. 3; 22. 14. 4; 23. 3. 2.

Appian *The Civil Wars* 5. 9.

Apuleius *Metamorphoses* [The Golden Ass] 8. 27; 11.

Arrian *Anabasis* 2. 13. 7–8; 2. 15. 6 to 2. 24. 6; 2. 25. 4; 7. 20. 1–2; 8. 20.

Athenaeus *The Deipnosophists* 9. 392d.

Augustine *Confessions* 6. 4. 5.

——— *Epistulae ad Romanos inchoata expositio* 13 (Migne, *PL* xxxv, 2096).

Clement of Alexandria *The Exhortation to the Greeks* 2. 25P.

Clement of Rome *The First Epistle to the Corinthians* 25.

Quintus Curtius *History of Alexander* 4. 6.

Dio Cassius *Roman History* 68. 31; 79. 8. 5; 80. 12. 1.

Diodorus Siculus *Bibliotheca* 2. 4. 1–3; 2. 48. 1–2, 4–5; 3. 43. 4; 19. 93–96; 20. 73. 3.

Eusebius *Ecclesiastical History* 1. 6. 2 and 1. 7. 11; 1. 13.

——— *Praeparatio evangelica* 1. 10. 7, 9, 16, 23, 31, 36–37.

Herodian *History* 5. 6. 3–5.

Herodotus *The Histories* 1. 105; 3. 5, 8; 4. 59; 6; 7. 98; 8. 67.

Homer *Iliad* 23. 740–745.

Flavius Josephus *Jewish Antiquities* 8. 35–36, 144–148 (*Contra Apionem* 1. 118–119); 9. 93, 283–285; 15. 253.

——— *The Jewish War* 1. 21. 11.

Julian *Epistulae* 298D–299A.

——— *Orationes* 4. 150CD, 154B; 7. 237A.

Julius Africanus in Eusebius *Ecclesiastical History* 1. 6. 2; 1. 7. 11.

Justin 1 *Apology* 4, 5.

Lucian of Samosata *De dea syria* passim.

——— *Icaromenippus* 25.

Macrobius *Saturnalia* 1. 23. 13; 3. 9.

Malalas *Chronicle* 8. 199. 2–4; 11. 280. 12–14.

Marcus the Deacon *The Life of Porphyry, Bishop of Gaza* 19–20.

Minutius Felix *Octavius* 18.

Nonus *Dionysiaca* 41. 68.

Origen *Contra Celsum* 1. 24–25; 4. 8, 98; 5. 25, 37; 8. 10–11.

Plato *Symposium* 181C.

——— *Timaeus* 28B.

Pliny the Elder *Naturalis historia* 5. 21. 86; 6. 29. 112.

Plutarch *De defectu oraculorum* 426BC.

Polybius *The Histories* 5. 79. 8.

Porphyry *De abstinentia* 2. 56.

Scriptores historiae augustae: Capitolinus *Clodius Albinus* 12. 12.

Seneca *Naturales quaestiones* 2. 45. 3.
Strabo *Geography* 14. 5. 2; 16. 1. 11, 27; 16. 4. 21, 23, 26, 27.
Suetonius *De vita Caesarum: Vespasianus* 5.
Suidas lexicographer s.v. *Theusares.*
Tacitus *Histories* 2. 78.
Tertullian *De anima* 2. 4.
——— *De idolatria* 15.
Xenophon *Anabasis* 1. 5.

4. Syriac and Arab Authors

"The Book of the Laws of Countries," in *Spicilegium syriacum,*
ed. W. Cureton (London, 1855). For the most recent edition,
see H.J.W. Drijvers, ed., *The Book of the Laws of Countries:
Dialogue on the Fate of Bardaiṣan of Edessa,* Semitic Texts
and Translations, III (Assen: Van Gorcum, 1965).
"Chronicle of Edessa," in I. Guidi, ed., *Chronica minora,* Corpus
scriptorum christianorum orientalium, Scriptores syri, ser. III,
vol. 4 (Paris, 1903), pp. 1–13.
"Discours de Jacques de Saroug sur la chute des idoles," Syriac
edition trans. into French and ed. P. Martin, *Zeitschrift der
Deutschen Morgenländischen Gesellschaft* 29 (1875), 107–147.
The Doctrine of Addai, the Apostle, Syriac edition with English
translation, ed. G. Phillips (London, 1876).
ibn-al-Kalbi, Hishām, *The Book of Idols,* trans. N. Amin Faris
(Princeton: Princeton University Press, 1952).
"'Oration of Meliton the Philosopher,' Known as the Homily of
Pseudo-Meliton of Sardis," in *Spicilegium syriacum,* ed. W.
Cureton (London, 1855), pp. 22–35 (text) and pp. 41–51
(English trans.), and in J. B. Pitra, *Spicilegium Solesmense,*
ed. E. Renan with Latin translation (Paris, 1885).
Theodore bar Koni, *Liber scholiorum,* ed. A. Scher, Corpus scrip-
torum christianorum orientalium, Scriptores syri, ser. II, vol.
66 (Paris, 1912).

5. Coins

Hill, G. F., *A Catalogue of the Greek Coins in the British Museum:
Phoenicia* (London, 1910).
———, *A Catalogue of the Greek Coins in the British Museum:
Palestine* (London, 1914).

Kadman, L., *The Coins of Akko-Ptolemais,* Corpus nummorum palaestinensium, IV (Tel Aviv: Schocken Publishing House, 1961).

Seyrig, H., "Divinités de Sidon," *Syria* 36 (1959), 48–56.

——, "Divinités de Ptolemais," *Syria* 39 (1962), 193–207.

——, "Questions aradiennes," *Revue numismatique* 6 (1964), 9–50.

——, "Le monnayage de Hiérapolis de Syrie à l'époque d'Alexandre," *Revue numismatique* 13 (1971), 11–21.

Walker, J., "The Coins of Hatra," *Numismatic Chronicle* 18 (1958), 167–172.

Wroth, W., *A Catalogue of the Greek Coins in the British Museum: Galatia* . . . (London, 1899).

6. Surveys, Excavation Reports, and Catalogues

Abel, F. M., "Les confins de la Palestine et de l'Égypte sous les Ptolémées," *Revue biblique* 48 (1939), 530–548.

Butler, H. C., *Architecture,* sect. A.: *Southern Syria,* Publications of the Princeton University Archaeological Expeditions to Syria in 1904–1905 and 1909, div. II (Leiden: E. J. Brill, 1919).

Collart, P., and J. Vicari, *Le sanctuaire de Baalshamin à Palmyre: Topographie et architecture,* Bibliotheca helvetica romana, X, 2 vols.: I, text, and II, plates (Neuchâtel: P. Attinger, 1969).

Cumont, F., *Fouilles de Doura-Europos (1922–1923),* Bibliothèque archéologique et historique, IX (Paris: Paul Geuthner, 1926).

Dunand, M., *Mission archéologique au Djebel Druze: Le Musée de Soueida,* Bibliothèque archéologique et historique, XX (Paris: Paul Geuthner, 1934).

——, and R. Duru, *Oumm el-ʿAmed,* see under no. 1, Semitic inscriptions: Phoenician and Punic.

Dussaud, R., *Topographie historique de la Syrie antique et médiévale,* Bibliothèque archéologique et historique, IV (Paris: Paul Geuthner, 1927).

——, and F. Macler, *Voyage,* see under no. 1, Semitic inscriptions: Collections of texts. . . .

Fellman, R., *Le sanctuaire de Baalshamin à Palmyre,* V: *Die Grabenlage,* Bibliotheca helvetica romana, X (Neuchâtel: P. Attinger, 1970).

Glueck, N., *Deities and Dolphins* (New York: Farrar, Straus and Giroux, 1965).

Ingholt, H., *Studier over palmyrensk Skulptur* (Copenhagen: Reitzel, 1928).

Karageorghis, V., "Fouilles de Kition," *Académie des Inscriptions et Belles-Lettres, Comptes rendus des séances de l'année 1969*, 515–522, and *Bulletin de correspondance hellénique* 94 (1970), 251–258, and 95 (1971), 379–386.

Krencker, D., and W. Zschietzschmann, *Römische Tempel in Syrien* (Berlin and Leipzig: W. de Gruyter, 1938).

Mesnil du Buisson, R. du, "Première campagne de fouilles à Palmyre," *Académie des Inscriptions et Belles-Lettres, Comptes rendus des séances de l'année 1966*, 158–190.

Musil, A., *The Northern Ḥeǧâz: A Topographical Itinerary* (New York: American Geographical Society, 1938).

Parr, P. J., G. L. Harding, and J. E. Dayton, "Preliminary Survey in N.W. Arabia, 1968," *Bulletin of the University of London Institute of Archaeology* 10 (1970), 23–61 [Nabataean inscriptions of J. T. Milik, pp. 54–57].

Peters, J. P., and H. Thiersch, *Painted Tombs in the Necropolis of Marissa* (London: Palestine Exploration Fund, 1905).

Rostovtzeff, M. I., F. E. Brown, and C. B. Welles, eds., *The Excavations at Dura-Europos: Preliminary Report of the Seventh and Eighth Seasons of Work, 1933–1934 and 1934–1935* (New Haven: Yale University Press, 1939).

Seyrig, H., "Ornamenta Palmyrena antiquiora," *Syria* 21 (1940), 277–328.

———, "Remarques sur la civilisation de Palmyre," *Syria* 21 (1940), 328–337.

Tesserae, see H. Ingholt et al. and R. du Mesnil du Buisson under no. 1, Semitic inscriptions: Palmyrene.

GENERAL INDEX

Aarras, 85
Abgal, a genie of the desert, 112
Abgar, king of Edessa, 148
Abiate, king of the Arabs, 67
Abibaal of Byblos, 47
Abirillu, 66
al-Abjaz, 62
abstemious god. *See* Nabataeans
Abu Kemal, 63
Abu Riğmen, 62
Acco, 19, 40, 51, 53
Acts of the Martyrs, 157
Acts of Thomas, 147n
Addu, Northwest Semitic deity, 53
Adiabene, 147, 148n
Adonai, 35, 125
Adonis, 35, 154, 155n
Adumatu, 64, 66
Aegeae, 56
Aelius Gallus, prefect of Egypt, 79
Aesculapius, 34, 44
Aglibol: the Moon god of Palmyra, 114–116, 120f, 141; and Malakbel, 108, 144. *See also* Palmyra
Ahab, king of Israel, 23, 56
Ahaz, king of Judah, 54
Ahiram of Byblos, 20
Ahura-Mazda, 29
Akhlamu, 22, 101
Akitu festival, 137
Akkar, 63
Aktab-Kutbâ, an Arab goddess, 155n
Aleppo, 31, 100
Alexander, 12, 40, 48, 52, 95; kept Persian administration in the Near East, 12

Alexander Jannaeus, 78
Alexander Severus, 56
Alexandria, 56, 153
Allat, 68f, 116n; theophorous names of, 158, 160
alphabet, origin of, 20
"Altar," a divine name, 86
altars: to the "anonymous" god of Palmyra, 122; to Baal Shamin, 130, 132f; dedication of, 6; in gold, 118; among the Nabataeans, 85–87; at Palmyra, 122, 135, 141, 144; at the spring Efca, 137; to Yarhibol, 111, 128
Amanus, 128n
Amashtart, 39
Amman, 35n
Ammianus Marcellinus, 33, 146f, 150f
Amorites, 101f, 111
Amrit, 34n
Amun, the Egyptian god, 21
Amurru, 101
Anat, 31
ancestral gods, 121, 128, 161–163; in Osrhoene, 149
angels: cult of, 14f, 38, 89; as messengers, 14, 162
"Anonymous" god, at Palmyra, 9f, 87, 122–130, 143
Anselm, St., *Proslogium*, 163
Antas (Sardinia), 41n, 119
Antigonus, 33, 52, 76f, 96
Anti-Lebanon, 32, 131
Antioch, 106
Antioch-by-the-Callirhoe, 146
Antiochia (Acco), 52
Antiochus III the Great, 52, 58, 104, 113

175

179

Ḥerembethel, 31, 86
Hermes, 69n, 88n
Hermon, see Mountain gods
Hermoupolis, 90; papyri of, 31, 86
Herod the Great, 52, 79f, 90, 97n
Herodian, on Elagabalus, 36n
Herodotus: on the Arabs, 68–70, 76; on Gaza and Ascalon as buffer zones, 95f; on the Tyrian fleet, 26
Herta, 116
Hierapolis, 47, 55, 59, 74
al-Ḥi jr (Madāin Ṣāliḥ), 67, 78f, 84, 87f
Hiram of Tyre, 20n, 23, 39
Historia augusta, 7, 33
Hit, 100
Holy, a Semitic epithet: Brothers, at Palmyra, 121, 126; cities, 51; garden, at Palmyra, 120f, 144; the - ones, 14n, 27; Prince, 39; Syrian goddess, 37; Zeus, at Baetocaece, 52
Holy Family, among the Phoenicians, 34, 39
Homs, 100
ḥštrpy, Šadrafa, equated with Apollo, 34n
ḥwrw, Nabataean settlement in Edom, 89f
hypsistos, 27, 123

ibn al-Kalbi, on Arabs and their idols, 73
Idalion, 8
Idaruma, the angel of Dushara, 15
idolatry, according to Christian writers, 152–155
idols, 38; in Arabia, 72–75; in North Syria, 152n; at Palmyra, 110f
Idumaea, 90f

Ilaalgé, 92
ilah, 83, 92
Iliad: description of the Phoenicians, 19
il (u), 83
"Image" of Baal, 48
immortality of the soul, 4f
impiety, defined by a Seleucid rescript, 50
Imtân, 82
incense route, 70, 73, 95
inscriptions: (in general), 3f, 5f, 8, 10f, 13f, 17, 26, 35, 42, 45, 161; Arabic, 64, 67; Aramaic, 8, 17, 31, 54; (Gözne, 141; Taima, 71ff; zkr of Hamath, 58, 141; Zinjirli, 150); bilingual of Rawwafa, 65n; Byblian, 47, 154n; Byblos, 22; Gezer, 20, 22; Greek, 20, 22, 35, 49f, 123n, 140; (Acco, 53, 55; Aradus, 49; Syria, 48); honorary, 45, 107n, 117f, 132; Latin, 50; (Dacia, 127n); Luwian hieroglyphs, 42; Mesha, 112; Nabataean, 29, 68, 79ff, 88ff, 92; (Delta, 68; Hauran, 88); North Syrian, 115n; Palmyrene, 9, 110, 125f, 130, 143; (earliest ones, 114; at Efca, 128; in Palmyrene, 75); Phoenician, 20, 23, 41, 44, 161; (Cyprus, 8, 20, 25, 37, 91, 154n); Punic, 22n, 119; Royal, 98, 161n; Safaitic, 70, 88; Syriac, 146, 149f; Ugaritic, 54
Ipsus, battle of, 33
Isamme clan, the, 67
Ishtar, 30, 36, 74, 116n; with the meaning of "goddess," 153n
Isis, 4, 7, 118n
Islam, 17, 73, 75, 163n
Israel, 23, 56; Israelites, 31, 37
Issus, battle of, 48
Ittobal of Sidon, 56.

INDEX OF AUTHORS

All the authors listed here appear in the footnotes

Library of Congress Cataloging in Publication Data

Teixidor, Javier.
  The pagan god.

  Bibliography: p.
  Includes index.
  1. Near East—Religion.   I. Title.
BL1060.T44   200′.956   76-24300
ISBN 0-691-07220-5